Gideon Welles

Lincoln and Seward

Remarks Upon the Memorial Address of Chas. Francis Adams, on the...

Gideon Welles

Lincoln and Seward
Remarks Upon the Memorial Address of Chas. Francis Adams, on the...

ISBN/EAN: 9783337009137

Printed in Europe, USA, Canada, Australia, Japan

Cover: Foto ©ninafisch / pixelio.de

More available books at **www.hansebooks.com**

LINCOLN AND SEWARD.

REMARKS UPON THE MEMORIAL ADDRESS OF CHAS.
FRANCIS ADAMS, ON THE LATE WM. H.
SEWARD,

WITH

*INCIDENTS AND COMMENTS ILLUSTRATIVE OF THE
MEASURES AND POLICY OF THE ADMINISTRA-
TION OF ABRAHAM LINCOLN,
AND VIEWS AS TO THE RELATIVE POSITIONS OF THE
LATE PRESIDENT AND SECRETARY
OF STATE.*

BY

GIDEON WELLES,
Ex-Secretary of the Navy.

NEW YORK:
SHELDON & COMPANY.
1874.

Entered according to Act of Congress in the year 1874, by
SHELDON & COMPANY,
in the Office of the Librarian of Congress at Washington.

Newburgh Stereotype Co.

PREFACE.

IN submitting the following pages, it is proper that the circumstances which led to, and attended their preparation, should go out with them. The "Memorial Address on the life, character and services of William H. Seward," which Mr. Adams delivered at Albany in April 1873, by invitation of the legislature of the State of New York, attracted general attention, and is a document which, if permitted to pass uncorrected, would be likely to contribute to, and strengthen false history. For a third of a century, Mr. Seward occupied prominent positions in his native state, and no inconsiderable space in the service of his country. It was appropriate that the state which had honored him with its confidence while living, should commemorate his death by an official observance such as the legislature ordered, and Mr. Adams was invited to fulfil. From a variety of considerations, the selection of the orator seemed proper; for there was much in his association with the deceased to commend it, and it opened a field of historic interest worthy of his pen. The extreme of panegyric, if the eulogist chose to indulge the partiality of friendship in that direction, was allowable and probably expected; but it was not anticipated that the occasion would be used to elevate the reputation of the deceased statesman at the expense of others, and certainly not by depreciating or underrating the abilities of the President under whom he served. The opportunity might have been improved to say a word in vindication of an administration which he had represented abroad, and of which Mr. Seward was a conspicuous member, for it had in the embittered contests of the period been greatly maligned, misrepresented, and misunderstood. No small disappointment was experienced to find the Address pregnant with error, and in some respects an indorsement of aspersions derogatory to President Lincoln and his capacity for the place he had filled, by representing that the merits and success of his administration were due, not to him, but to the superior intellectual power of the Secretary of State.

My first impression on reading the Address was, that the surviving members of Mr. Lincoln's Cabinet should unite in a general statement correcting the misrepresentations semi-officially put forth at Albany. Such a statement from them, brief and decisive, without details, would probably have been sufficient to counteract the misrepresentations and erroneous assertions of Mr. Adams, as to the relative merits, executive ability and individual services of the President and Secretary of State during Mr. Lincoln's administration. Some correspondence in regard to such a proceeding took place between Messrs. Chase, Blair, and myself, which was interrupted by the sudden death of the Chief Justice within less than one month after the Address was delivered. This event rendered it advisable that something more should be done than a mere contradictory assertion, or naked statement that Mr. Adams was mistaken in his estimate of the two men and their relative positions to each other, and to their associates in the administration, as well as to the whole conduct of the affairs of the government.

Of the eight persons who constituted the Executive Council, and administered the government during the dark days of our country's December, four, besides the two eminent characters adverted to in the Memorial Address, had closed their earthly pilgrimage. Only two members of the Cabinet who first met around that councilboard, and conferred together through most of the years of President Lincoln's Administration, survived to speak from personal knowledge of the acts, qualifications and services of their chief, and those with whom they had been associated in that trying period.

By special request of Mr. Blair, the duty of stating the facts and vindicating Mr. Lincoln and his administration from the errors or inadvertencies of Mr. Adams devolved on me. To discharge that duty with fidelity was a delicate and embarrassing task, lest in developing the facts in regard to the conduct and measures of the administration, and repelling the remarks derogatory to President Lincoln, it might seem that injustice was done to Secretary Seward, to whom credit as a superior to the President in native intellectual power, and in the force of moral discipline, and as directing affairs in the President's name, had been awarded. But while maintaining for Mr. Lincoln greater executive ability, I would withhold no just fame from Mr. Seward, whose versatile and prolific mind, if less persistent and reliable, less capable of establishing and enforcing a policy, less capable of grasping great questions and successfully wielding the highest functions of government, was nevertheless in his position, active, industrious and useful. If disclosures of the truth dispel prevailing error, let it not be supposed that wrong is thereby done to a colleague for whom I had great personal regard.

Undoubtedly both Mr. Adams and Mr. Seward believed in 1860, that Mr. Lincoln possessed neither the abilities nor qualifications to perform the duties of Chief Magistrate, and that he would consequently be governed by some leading member of his Cabinet. It was assumed by them, and indeed by others, that the Secretary of State would be that leading member and President, de facto. Mr. Seward after a brief experience, learned his mistake. Mr. Adams never did—nor does it appear that Mr. Seward, in their intimate personal and official correspondence undeceived or enlightened the Minister during his absence from the country, covering the entire presidency of Mr. Lincoln. Besides, a class of partisans in all that time busied themselves in affirming and inculcating the false impression that Mr. Seward was the actual Executive. John Wilkes Booth, like Mr. Adams was deceived by it, and hence in his scheme to overturn and destroy the government, he deemed it essential to make Mr. Seward, as well as the President a victim. The murderous attempt of a crazy fanatic, gave strength to the delusion which partisans had promulgated. Sympathy for the survivor of that terrible catastrophe, who, wounded and mangled, escaped the knife of the assassin, seemed to identify him more closely with his chief who had been slain, and, temporarily at least, added to the delusion which finds endorsement and is embodied in the Memorial Address.

In the following pages I have confined my remarks as far as possible, to the acts, views and transactions of the President and Secretary of State and measures of administration during the presidency of Mr. Lincoln. Allusions to other periods, or to the private life or peculiar characteristics of either, except as preliminary or essential to a correct understanding of their official career, and political principles have been avoided. In stating the views and policy of Mr. Lincoln, it has been no part of my purpose to discuss the labors or services of Mr. Seward, other than those which relate to the administration of which he was a member, not the chief. Whatever estimate may be put upon his abilities— whatever resemblance there may have been between him and the renowned men of antiquity, or the distinguished statesmen of our own country of a past generation, or whatever may have been his experience in other years, and in different fields of public, professional, or social life, are proper matters of eulogy, but foreign to the purpose of these remarks.

Incidents and measures which occurred, better than statements or assertions, will disabuse the public mind and more truly than mere declarations develop the characteristics of the men and the workings of the administration. I have therefore selected certain cases on different topics, which denote the ideas, executive ability and principles of government of the President and Secretary of State on questions of public policy. They also indicate the actual relation in which they stood to each other, and their associates in the Cabinet. The cases mentioned relate to by-gone measures which have been adjusted or disposed of, and are parts of the recorded, though to some extent, unpublished history of the country and times.

The remarks on the Address as originally prepared were too voluminous for a Magazine. I therefore condensed and reduced them to three papers which appeared in the Galaxy for October, November and December 1873. The reception of those papers by the public, led the publishers and others to request that the numbers which had appeared, and the whole of the omitted portions with attending details and such additions as I thought proper, might be embodied in a volume, which is herewith submitted.

G. W.

Mr. Lincoln and Mr. Seward.

IT is to be regretted that Mr. Charles Francis Adams, in his "Memorial Address on the Life, Character, and Services of William H. Seward," should have permitted himself to do injustice to Abraham Lincoln. Any attempt to canonize Mr. Seward by detracting from the merits of his chief weakens the encomiums bestowed. Mr. Adams has claims to consideration by reason of his talents, acquirements, social position, and public service; but his estimate of the character, capacity, executive ability, and relative position of the Chief Magistrate and his Secretary of State betrays a want of just discrimination and correct knowledge of each. A greater error could scarcely be committed than to represent that Mr. Lincoln "had to deal with a superior intelectual power" when he came in contact with Mr. Seward. The reverse was the fact. In mere scholastic acquirements "Mr. Seward, never a learned man," may have had the advantage, though in this respect there was less difference than is generally supposed; while "in breadth of philosophical experience and in the force of moral discipline" the almost self-taught and reflective mind of Mr. Lincoln, which surmounted difficulties and disadvantages that his Secretary never knew, conspicuously excelled. In the executive council and in measures of administration the Secretary had influence, not always happily exercised; but the President's was the master mind. It is empty panegyric to speak of the Secretary of State as chief, or to say his suggestions, save in his own department, were more regarded or had even greater influence than those of others. His restless activity, unceasing labors, showy manifestations, and sometimes incautious exercise of questionable authority which the President deemed it impolitic to disavow, led to the impression, which Mr. Adams seems also to have imbibed, that the subordinate was the principal, and have induced him, to use his own words, to "award to one honors that clearly belong to another."

Far be it from me to derogate in the least from the merits and services of Mr. Seward, for I was a witness to his assiduity, and to some extent a participant and coadjutor with him in the labors and trials that the Administration encountered in troublous times. But it was not necessary in stating his merits, even in eulogy, to undervalue and misstate the worth, services, and capabilities of the remarkable man who was at the helm and guided the Government through a stormy period. Unassuming and unpretentious himself, Mr. Lincoln was the last person to wear borrowed honors. He was not afflicted with the petty jealousy of narrow minds, nor had he any apprehension that others would deprive him of just fame. He gave to Mr. Seward, as to each of his council, his generous confidence, and patiently listened, if he did not always adopt or assent to the suggestions that were made. To those who knew Abraham Lincoln, or who were at all intimate with his Administration, the representation that he was subordinate to any member of his Cabinet, or that he was deficient in executive or administrative ability, is absurd. Made on a solemn occasion as was this address, and published and sent out to the world in a document which purports to be not only eulogistic but historic, it is essential that the errors thus spread abroad should be corrected. Mr. Adams had not an intimate acquaintance with Mr. Lincoln, and evidently but a slight general knowledge of his character. With admitted great disappointment and disgust, he, in May 1861, received the intelligence that this lawyer, legislator, and political student of the praries, whom he did not know and with whom he had not associated, had been preferred by the Republican representatives at Chicago over a Senator from the Empire State with whom he was intimate and familiar, who had long official experience, which he seems to have considered essential, was acquainted with legislative management, and whose political and party sympathies accorded with his own. His prejudices as well as his partiality were excited, and from the beginning he misconceived the character and undervalued and underrated the capabilities and qualities of one of the most sagacious and remarkable men of the age.

In his statements of the political career of Mr. Seward, and of the structure and condition of parties from the days of the Monroe administration, one is compelled to believe the eulogist has, as he expresses it, plunged in "the Serbonian bog of obsolete party politics." Yet politics and parties are an essential part of the history of the country, its men and the times, and the author himself has made politics the study of his life. Mr. Seward was also emphatically a party politician. He had a fondness for political studies and employment, and was at all times active and faithful in the service of each of the several political parties to which he belonged. Whether "the chief characteristic of his mind was its breadth of view" may be questioned by some who look to his general course and form their opinion of his "characteristics" from it and his acts. If not, as is asserted, a "philosopher studying politics," he was kind and affable, of a genial temperament, calm and subdued under reverses, and to his credit never manifested the malevolence and acerbity which too often characterize intense political partisans. Among his party associates he always occupied a decidedly prominent place, by reason of his sociability and urbanity as well as of his ability. He was quick of apprehension, prolific in suggestions and expedients, and endowed, if not with eloquence or a commanding presence, with a readiness and facility of expression in speech or writing which enabled him in consultations, and when associated with others, to carry personal influence equal to any, and much greater than most of his contemporaries. He had not, however, an executive mind which could of itself magnetize and subordinate others, or the mental strength to take the helm and steadily guide and direct the policy of the government or of a party. Henry Clay once said, "Mr. Seward is a man of no convictions." This may not have been strictly true, yet he was not a man of fixed principles, whose convictions would not yield to circumstances or be modified by expedients, some of which might be scarcely worthy of consideration. He could be as tenacious as any in adhering to a measure or policy so long as his associates, or those friends in whom he trusted, maintained the position; but alone, he had not the will, self-reliance, and obstinancy to plant himself on the rock of principle, meet the storm, and abide the consequences.

Mr. Seward was a politician—a partisan politician of the central school—with talents more versatile than profound; was more of a conservative than a reformer, with no great original conceptions of right, nor systematic ideas of administration. So far as his party adopted a reforming policy he went with it, and he was with it also in opposing actual reforms by the Democrats. The representation that he was a veteran reformer, or the leader of the anti-slavery movement or of the Republican party, is a mistake. He was neither an Abolitionist nor a Free-soiler, nor did he unite with the Republicans until the Whig party virtually ceased to exist in most of the states, and was himself one of the last to give up that party, of which he had been from its commencement and in all its phases an active member. It was with reluctance he finally yielded, when the feeble remnant of that organization disbanded. The Republican party, with which he then became associated, was not of mushroom growth. It was years maturing. Mr. Seward, whose friends claim for him its paternity, was a Whig at its inception. He neither rocked its cradle nor identified himself with its youth, but gave it cheering words, as he had other ephemeral organizations, in order to weaken the Democrats and help the Whigs. Faithful to party, he adhered to the Whigs under all circumstances. It was his marked public characteristic. Not until the Whig party was prostrate—a skeleton without strength or vitality—did he yield and embark his political fortunes in the great uprising. In the destruction of the political scaffolding which he and his friends had constructed, perished the hopes and labors of years. To relinquish the machinery and organization which by lobby management under a skilful leader had become powerful and controlling in the Empire State of the Union, was a sacrifice not willingly made, and when made it was not in the anti-slavery interest, but with a covert design to perpetuate the Albany dynasty under the name of Republican. The Albany lobby was never an abolitionist lobby or an anti-slavery lobby, nor was the organization or its candidate. Any attempt to represent him, or those associated with him, as occupying a more advanced position on the anti-slavery question than those who were of the "Jefferson school," is rather eulogy than fact. In the presidential contest of 1848, when the domination of previously existing parties was broken, and a stand was made against the expansion of slavery and its extension into the territories from which it had been excluded, Mr. Seward delined to connect himself with the Free-soil or Anti-slavery cause, but clung to the Whig party which opposed the movement, and voted for a candidate who was a slave-owner in preference to a statesman and citizen of his own State who was not.

According to Mr. Adams, " the origin of the division of parties which prevailed for more than thirty years," began about the close of the first quarter of the present century, soon after the adoption of the Missouri compromise, consequently in the opening years of Mr. Seward's manhood and political life. " At the outset of Mr. Seward's career," says the address, " the first thing necessary for him to do was to choose his side. Under his father's roof the influences naturally carried him to sympathize with the old Jeffersonian party on the one hand, while the relics of the slave system remaining in the family as house-servants, the least repulsive form of that relation seemed little likely to inspire in him much aversion to it on the other. Nevertheless he early formed his conclusions adversely to the organization in New York professing to be the successors of the Jeffersonian school, and not less so to the perpetuation of slavery any where. The reason for this is obvious. With his keen perception of the operation of general principles he penetrated at once the fact that the resurrection in this form of the old party was not only hollow but selfish. It looked to him somewhat like a close corporation made for the purpose of dealing in popular doctrines, not so much for the public benefit as for that of the individual directors. Moreover it became clear that among those doctrines, that of freedom to the slave was rigorously excluded by reason of the bond of union entered into with his master at the south. In reality, he was in principle too democratic for the democrats. Hence he waged incessant war against this form of oligarchy down to the hour when it was finally broken up."

In addition to this fact or fancy sketch, Mr. Adams says that in a Fourth of July oration delivered by Mr. Seward at Auburn when he was twenty-four years old, he made "the *deliberate claim of a right in the Federal government to emancipate slaves by legislation,*" and that "in his conclusions he proved a prophet." Jefferson, though sincerely opposed to slavery, was not of the prophets or politicians who made claim to any such right in the Federal government. Had he made such claims, or believed that there was any such authority or principle in the government, his love of freedom was so great, and his principles and convictions so abiding he would never have advised its relinquishment, or consented that the government and people should be forever bound by a fundamental law incorporated into the constitution and made unrepealable prohibiting legislation through all time whatever, in the progress of human affairs might be the opinions and wishes of the people. But Mr. Seward who we are told "waged incessant war against this form of oligarchy down to the hour when it was finally broken up," was ready when sixty years old to manacle Congress and, so far as the Federal government was concerned, to consign the slaves to perpetual bondage. In his carefully elaborated and celebrated speech delivered on the twelfth of January 1861, he said: "I am willing to vote for an amendment to the constitution declaring that it shall not, by any future amendment, be so altered as to confer on Congress a power to abolish or interfere with slavery in any state." It is for the author of the Memorial Address who speaks of incessant war against the slave-oligarchy down to the hour when it was finally broken up, to reconcile the claim put forth by Mr. Seward when twenty-four years old, that the Federal government had a right to emancipate by legislation, with his willingness after forty years experience and study of the government, to surrender any such claim or right forever.

The disposition of the financial and tariff questions which for years divided parties under renowned leaders, and the Mexican war with its results during the Polk administration, affected the political status of individuals and also the organization of parties. Clay, Calhoun, and Webster, the intellectual and imperious triumvirate who combined against Jackson fifteen years before, were each infirm from increasing years, and on the descending grade of life and influence. In 1849 they retained, individually, but a feeble hold on their followers. Van Buren and Benton were no longer formidable. With the departure of old questions, the old contestants were passing away. It was just at this period, when old political parties were in a fragmentary and transition state, that Mr. Seward first entered the national councils as a Senator from the great State of New York. No time could have been more propitious or circumstances more favorable for a genuine reformer—a statesman of mental grasp and real executive talent, sincere in his convictions and wedded to principle, with the advantage of high position, to have gathered up, concentrated and organized the disturbed political elements which were dissatisfied with government abuses and central aggressive power in behalf of an institution which was tolerated but disliked, and its extension and aggressions resisted. This was an opportunity for a statesman, in place if possessed of the indispensable executive ability, to have made himself the leader of a great movement. But Mr. Seward did not prove himself equal to the position. He was still a Whig and failed to raise the standard and rally the host. In opposing the assumptions of a civil aggression, he was one with others, not their superior nor their chief. Though quick of apprehension and not insensible to the new aspect of affairs and the change that was taking place, he had neither the resolution nor the inclination to abandon his party, "break up the remnants of party ties," and place himself at the head of a popular demonstration for immortal principles. He had been a life-long party follower —had trod the paths and ruts of party obediently and faithfully, and been so trained and disciplined, so accustomed to look up to others to decide and lead, that no will or independence was left him at fifty to take the initiative in a new departure. He had the sagacity to see that new questions were entering into our politics and old ones were becoming obsolete, but possessed not the courage to abandon the old, nor the organizing and executive talent to become the chief in a new movement. Contrary to good instruction and sound principle, he and the Albany managers attempted to put this new Republican wine into old Whig bottles, under the delusive idea that the effete and decaying Whig organization could receive and hold this fermenting political element without bursting. He made able speeches on the rising questions, as did others; but the Senate produced no commanding mind, with "clarion voice" and magnetic power, to rally and lead. Mr. Seward had adventitious advantages above others which his associates felt and conceded. He had been Governor of the largest State in the Union, was its representative in Congress, and stood the peer of any of his associates on the floor of the Senate, but only the peer. Neither in Congress nor subsequently in the Cabinet did he display the administrative or executive talent that was anticipated, or which partisan admirers claim for him at the expense of Mr. Lincoln.

In closing his "Memorial Address" Mr. Adams alludes to the friends of Mr. Seward, and particularly one who survives, "whose singularly disinterested labor has been to effect the elevation of others to power, and never his own; and to whose remarkable address I strongly suspect Mr. Seward owed many obligations of that kind." No person in the least conversant with the two men could have heard or read the address without a conviction, even if no acknowledgment had been made, that the spirit of the friend inspired and imbued the orator with the partialities, prejudices, misconceptions, and errors which pervade the address and are manifest on almost every page.

Mr. Thurlow Weed, who for forty years was the ruling mind of the party with which he was associated in New York, possessed remarkable qualities as a party manager. The character and services of Mr. Seward can never be delineated or understood without mention of this *alter ego*, who was not only his *fidus Achates*, but it may without disparagement be said was also, with some radical failings, his *Mentor*. Mr. Weed, a man of strong, rough native intellect, without much early culture, was a few years the senior of Mr. Seward, whose more polished and facile mind adapted itself to the other—clung to it as the ivy to the oak—and the two became inseparable in politics. When Mr. Seward was about to "choose his side," Weed was the editor of a paper in western New York, which fomented the wild, fanatical, and proscriptive antimasonic excitement that for a brief period swept with uncontrollable and unreasoning fury that section of country. An organized party was formed on the narrow basis of hate, intolerance, and proscription of every man who belonged to the Masonic fraternity, every one of whom was to be excluded from office, from the jury-box and all places of trust. Under this anti-masonic banner, of which Weed was a champion leader, Mr. Seward enlisted and commenced his public official career, was its candidate in that district, and elected by that party to the Senate of New York. Many will believe that he did not manifest great "breadth of view," nor prove himself a profound "philosopher studying politics," nor display the "capacity to play a noble part on the more spacious theatre of State affairs," when he entered the Senate of New York an anti-masonic partisan under the guidance of Thurlow Weed. But the friendship commenced under those auspices continued unabated to the death of the junior, and evinces itself in the "Memorial Address" which attempts to place Mr. Seward above the President to whom he was subordinate, and "award to him honors that clearly belong to another."

Mr. Weed possessed capacity which rightly directed might have been of service to the country and to mankind. He was not without good qualities when party and personal favorites or opponents were not concerned; but he was wanting in political morality, and was unscrupulous in his party intrigues—often and without hesitation resorting to schemes to carry a measure in the Legislature, or to secure an election, which scarcely savored of political or moral honesty.

When the anti-masonic fervor subsided and the organization died out, Messrs. Seward and Weed became identified with the opponents of the Jackson administration and the supporters of "the American system"—a centralizing policy. The address represents that "the political unity of the country under its present form of government naturally divides itself into two periods of nearly equal length." One, which commenced with Washington and closed with Monroe, related chiefly to questions of foreign policy. The other was on the subject of slavery. There is no such natural division. The statement is neither politically nor historically correct, but an arbitrary assumption, warranted by neither history nor facts. The slavery question in no form or shape entered into the election or administration of General Jackson or the great parties of that period. Other absorbing subjects, relating to the bank, to finance, to the tariff and internal improvements, combined under what in the party nomenclature of the day was styled the "American system," were the political and party issues for a quarter of a century succeeding the Monroe administration. It was then, "at the outset of Mr. Seward's career," when there was no controversy or difference in State or national parties or politics on the subject of slavery that Weed and "the philosopher studying politics," chose their side, opposed Jackson, supported Clay, advocated a national bank, a protective tariff, internal improvements by the federal government, and the whole centralizing "American system." There was no identification of either of the great opposing parties of that day with slavery or anti-slavery. From 1828, when Jackson was elected, to the election of Taylor in 1848, neither party made the subject of slavery a test question, or part of its political creed. Opposition to General Jackson and his administration, and to the policy initiated under him, to state rights and constitutional limitations, combined the adverse elements and was the ground-work of the Whig party, to which in all its phases Mr. Seward was a devoted adherent. A coalition was formed by the Whigs with the nullifiers, who were slave-holders, and at a later day secessionists, against the patriotic old chieftain who put forth the executive power for the maintenance of the federal union. But the tariff, not slavery, was the pretext for nullification, and opposition to the administration was the apology for a compromise in which both the protectionists and nullifiers surrendered each their principles.

Then, and until some time past the meridian of his life—a period of more than twenty years—Mr. Seward was, for reasons doubtless satisfactory to himself, one of the most zealous and active party men in the country. With him every side-issue, every controverted question, every element of discontent against the government, was courted, fanned, favored, and made subservient to party. This embraces the period when, according to the address, Mr. Seward chose his side adversely to the organization of the Jefferson school, was "too democratic for the Democrats," was "far more practical than anything ever taught by Jefferson." This peculiar democracy and anti-masonry constitute what the address describes as "the various phenomena of Mr. Seward's public life," but which his contemporaries understood to be political partnership of a very active and decided character. In New York and throughout the country Mr. Seward was known and recognized as a busy and efficient party man in the Whig organization, and one of the leaders to whom the party in that state was under obligation for partisan services. His sphere of influence was limited to his state, for beyond its borders the corrupt Albany lobby led and managed by Weed was detested by the Democrats and distrusted by the Whigs themselves. Whatever abilities or qualities of mind he possessed—and they were in some respects remarkable—were given earnestly and cheerfully to that party and its centralizing "American system" policy. In their party councils in New York, Thurlow Weed became the supreme manager, and guiding, controlling spirit, always declining office. Mr. Seward was the orator or oracle, and received the official honors. When anti-masonry was on the wane, and after Mr. Seward entered the New York Senate, Weed removed to Albany, where he established a paper and exercised with skill and effect his love of intrigue. He soon organized and became chief of a lobby which had an odious notoriety, and which, while it gave him a certain influence in New York, was viewed with abhorrence by many, with distrust by the whole country. His management was, however, adroit; and the lobby under his direction, though often profligate, unscrupulous, and always debauching and corrupting, contributed at times largely to the success of his party and the promotion of Mr. Seward. The personal influence of Weed was enhanced and made effective by his apparent self-abnegation and uniform and persistent refusal to accept any office himself, while all around him were seeking office and legislative favors. His labors were not as disinterested as represented; for if he declined place he loved power, and it was his pride and ambition to manage the government of New York when the Whigs were successful and in the ascendant, to say who might hold office, to control measures, and to prescribe the policy and direct the movements of his party—not always perhaps judiciously or honestly in either respect; but the administration in that State, its measures and men, were nevertheless his. The mental force, magnetism, system, and will of the man were artful, but imperious and indisputable with his party, yet were shrewdly and in general discreetly exercised. Mr. Seward, ever preadvised and consulted, was his exponent in the Legislature and in party councils, and the advocate or opponent of the measures and men as prescribed, with his concurrence by Weed. Although the latter never sought office for himself, he always wanted high place for Seward, who was his cherished and almost idolized political offspring, with whom he never disagreed, and who never went counter to him. The two always acted in concert. It was interesting to witness their joint operations. Weed's mind had by far the greatest vigor, Seward's the most pliability. It was so in their anti-masonic days. It was so to the close. Weed's apparently disinterested labors were selfish, yet given with devoted and unsparing fidelity to his friend Seward, who might wear the honors while he was the substantial power behind. Their ideas of government were always personal, when their party was in power they were the state. Mr. Adams "strongly suspects 'Mr. Seward owed many obligations" to Mr. Weed. It was never suspicion among those who knew them, but an unquestioned and indisputable fact. Mr. Seward himself acknowledged it with apparent satisfaction. I once heard him declare, others being present, "Seward is Weed and Weed is Seward. What I do, Weed approves. What he says, I endorse. We are one." "I am sorry to hear the remark," said the late Chief Justice Chase, "for while I would strain a point to oblige Mr. Seward, I feel under no obligations to do anything for the special benefit of Mr. Weed. The two are not and never can be one to me."

Mr. Adams declares, as historical truth:

"The fact is beyond contradiction that no person ever before nominated, with any reasonable probability of success had so little of public service to show for his reward. . . . The President elect was [in the winter of 1861] still at home in Illinois giving no signs of life. . . That which appeared most appalling was the fact that we were to have for our guide through this perilous strife a person selected partly on account of the absence of positive qualities, so far as was known to the public, and absolutely without the advantage of any experience in national affairs, beyond the little that can be learned by an occupation of two years in the House of Representatives. . . . . It was clear, at least to me, that our chance of success would rest upon an executive council composed of the wisest and most experienced men that could be found. So it seemed absolutely indispensable on every account that not only should Mr. Seward have been early secured in a prominent post, but that his advice at least should have been asked in regard to the completion of that organization. But Mr. Lincoln as, yet knew little of all this. His mind had not even opened to the nature of the contest. From his secluded home in the heart of Illinois, he was only taking measure of his geographical relations and party services, and beginning his operations where others commonly leave off, at the smaller end. Hence, it was at quite a late period of the session before he had disclosed his intention to put Mr. Seward in the most prominent place. . . . It is the duty of history, in dealing with all human events, to do strict justice in discriminating between persons, and by no means to award to one honors that clearly belong to another. I must then affirm, without hesitation, that in the history of our government, down to this hour, no experiment so rash has ever been made as that of elevating to the head of affairs a man with so little previous preparation for his task as Mr. Lincoln. . . . . Mr. Lincoln could not fail soon to perceive the fact that whatever estimate he might put on his own natural judgment, he had to deal with a superior in native intellectual power, in extent of acquirement, in breadth of philosophic experience, and in the force of moral discipline. On the other hand, Mr. Seward could not have been long blind to the deficiencies of his chief in these respects."

Those who read and give credit to these representations, and others of similar purport through the address, will receive very erroneous impressions of the two men to whom they relate, as well as of the administration to which they belonged, and in which each bore an important part. It was not Mr. Lincoln who conformed himself and his policy and general views to Mr. Seward, but it was Mr. Seward who adapted himself with ease and address to Mr. Lincoln, and, failing to influence, adopted and carried out the opinions and decisions of his chief. In that respect—flexibility and facility of change among friends—no person possessed greater dexterity and tact than the Secretary of State. It made him a pleasant assistant, companion, and coadjutor; but his character not being positive, nor his convictions absolute, he was not always reliable, being deficient in executive will and ability. Mr. Lincoln, who is represented as ignorant of the condition of the country when elected, and " whose mind had not yet opened to the nature of the crisis," better understood, if we may judge from what they did, the popular sentiment and the public requirements than senator or representative, ambassador or cabinet minister. In his " secluded home" he was not an inattentive and indifferent observer, but watched and studied public measures and public necessities, and more correctly appreciated the actual condition of affairs than the heated politicians engaged in factious strife for party ascendency in the national and state capitals. While statesmen and legislators of "experience" in Congress were waiting and watching for new appointments, neglectful of the coming storm, anticipating apparently little else than a severe party conflict, "utterly without spirit" to concert measures —exhausting their time and energies in frivolous wragnles, and accomplishing nothing—with confessedly "no leader at hand equal" to the emergency—the President elect, "in the heart of Illinois," comprehended the situation, and rose above merely personal and party contentions to the dangers, necessities and political condition of the country. Wholly powerless, however, he was compelled to witness without being able to prevent the disintegration in progress, and the accumulating embarrassments that were soon to confront him, without a single effective demonstration from any of his professed friends in Congress, who prided themselves on their superiority, and on an official "experience" in which they deemed him deficient, but which experience they considered indispensable for a competent executive. Of what value was the "experience" of senator or representative in that crisis? What executive or legislative ability did they exhibit? Experience rightly improved is valuable in public official life, but it is not to be denied that it often blunts the mind, and by familiarizing with, renders it indifferent to evil.

The two great parties of Democrat and Whig were in their day scarcely more apart in their character or more diverse in their purposes than the opposing elements which met in convention at Chicago in 1860. It was by no means a personal contest as represented.

Mr. Adams seems unconscious of the fact that there were among Republicans, and in that convention, conflicting views and policies; that a majority was opposed to corrupt legislation and the vicious schemes of managing lobbies, whether at Albany or Washington, as well as hostile to the extension and aggression of slavery. It was the misfortune of Mr. Seward that he was associated with and the candidate of the most offensive lobby combination of that date. He was not accused or suspected of receiving pecuniary benefit himself from the practices of that class of jobbing party lobbyists, but he was thought to be indifferent if not assenting to their practices, and was their candidate. They were active in his favor, were conspicuously instrumental in pressing him forward as the coming man, announcing him as the Republican candidate, and used extraordinary means to secure delegates to the nominating convention in his interest. These party managers had, like Mr. Seward, adhered to the Whig organization so long as it existed. After its abandonment they became active members of the Republican party, and strove to be foremost in all its proceedings. But there was a large element—the result showed a very decided majority—of the Republicans averse to any nomination or movement which would tend to transfer Albany intrigues to Washington, and introduce the debasing practices on the Hudson into our national politics.

When the convention met at Chicago, the Albany programme and management were obvious. New York and Michigan, under the Whig machinery which with all its appliances was still in force in those states though under the name of Republicanism, pushed solidly for their candidate. Massachusetts was supposed to have been as thoroughly attended to, but a small minority dissented and went with the majority of the states and delegates from New England in opposition to Mr. Seward. These three states constituted his substantial strength, but under Albany manipulation and management some of the small frontier and border states, and the territories which were introduced and permitted to vote in convention, though they could not in election, added to his force, and gave him, as the address states, a plurality on the first ballot. A second ballot increased his vote but eleven, when it was evident the Albany programme could not succeed, and the whole personal intrigue was demolished. The lobby measures and tactics, and all the dramatic parade and performance in the streets and hotels of Chicago, failed. Disappointed and overwhelmed, Weed refused to return to New York, but left for the Northwest, and some days later made his appearance far south at Springfield, where he had an interview with Mr. Lincoln in "his secluded abode." It was with *fidus Achates* still a personal matter, and if Mr. Seward could not be President he wished him in a position where he could be potential in the coming administration, believing with Mr. Adams that Mr. Lincoln had "little previous preparation for his task," and that Mr. Seward was his superior in "native intellectual power." A very serious mistake on the part of both. Members of Congress had also expected, and took it for granted, that a man in official position and of political experience, with hereditary party claims, and a personal following as well as pecuniary backers, such as could be found only in the commercial metropolis, would be selected. Others, however, wished a liberal candidate, wedded to no past organization, and untainted by and wholly disconnected with legislative or congressional corruption and intrigue.

Mr. Lincoln became the choice of the convention, not only from a belief that he had ability for the place, but because he was a Republican from the start, a private citizen, honest sagacious, and firm, with no vicious connections or debasing political associations or antecedents. It was not " the ghosts of the higher law and of the irrepressible conflict " which made Mr. Lincoln a candidate, for he and Mr. Seward stood alike in that respect ; nor was it " the element of bargain and management manipulated by adepts at intrigue " which secured his nomination, for the " adepts at intrigue" were active for another.

The convention and the people preferred Abraham Lincoln, in what Mr. Adams calls " his secluded abode in the heart of Illinois " to Senator Seward, with all his experience and metropolitan surroundings, because he was more truly the representative of the Republican movement. Nor did the country regret, or ever have cause to regret, that preference, whatever may have been the disgust of disappointed officials and expectants in Washington or elsewhere. Time, and trials far greater than have ever been the lot of any other chief magistrate, tested and proved the wisdom of their choice. Mr. Lincoln, honest, intelligent, deliberate, patriotic, and determined, if not courtly bred, had the executive ability to guide the ship of state through a pitiless storm. Mr. Seward, with his restless flexible mind, prolific in expedients, but with no well-defined policy, fixed political principles, or strong tenacity of purpose, could not have wielded the executive power successfully, or navigated the ship of state in safety at that period, could he have been nominated and elected, of which last there are very grave doubts. There have been previous occasions, as in 1828 and again in 1840, when all the calculations of politicians, statesmen of experience, and men in place, have been wrecked by an upheaval of popular sentiment, and candidates taken from the ranks—"secluded abodes"— were carried forward on the mighty wave of public, if sometimes mistaken, opinion to a triumphant election.

Mr. Adams fails to mention, and probably never realized, the primary differences in the Republican party which caused results so unexpected to him and the politicians in Congress. It was confidently expected that the six Eastern states which had been the stronghold of the whig party and where the central organization was powerful, would concentrate on Mr. Seward, but though many of the party leaders were committed to his support he was never a favorite with the people. No manipulation or appliances could secure him their support. On the first ballot at Chicago, Connecticut, Rhode Island and Vermont were unanimous against him—New Hampshire gave him only one of her twelve votes. Maine and Massachusetts were divided. The delegates were committed to no one of the several candidates but were decided against Mr. Seward. Before the convention met, it was supposed that an arrangement could be made with Cameron, by which Pennsylvania could be brought in to sustain Mr. Seward, but although that politician's influence was great it was totally insufficient to attach Pennsylvania to the Albany movement.

So unaware was Mr. Seward of the true condition of things when the convention assembled at Chicago —so convinced that the Albany programme would succeed—that he left his seat in the Senate and repaired to Auburn in the confident expectation of there receiving a committee which would inform him of his nomination. The adverse blow was severe; but more readily than many of his friends, did he submit to the great disappointment, and with his usual tact accepted and acquiesced in results which he could not control.

The "Memorial Address" represents it to have been an error that Mr. Seward was not "early secured in a prominent post" by the President elect, and says that "his advice at least should have been asked in regard to the completion of the organization." The reverse of this was a matter of duty, for the views and wishes of Mr. Seward and his special friends were not the policy and intention of Mr. Lincoln and the Republicans. Mr. Lincoln knew that the services of Mr. Seward were at his disposal in case the Republicans were successful, even before he was elected, and it was impressed upon him most earnestly as a necessity immediately thereafter. Twice at least did Thurlow Weed, the faithful managing friend of Mr. Seward, the *fidus Achates* "to whom he owed many obligations of that kind," visit Springfield in Mr. Seward's behalf. The views of Mr. Lincoln in regard to the composition of his executive council, and the material of which it should be constructed, were so widely different from those of Mr. Seward and his Albany associates, that no inclination was felt to ask his or their advice on the subject. He had the selection of Mr. Seward in his mind as early as that of any of his associates, but he had no more thought of consulting him as regarded the other members of his Cabinet than of advising with them or either of them as to his Secretary of State. The members were to be his advisers, not Mr. Seward's; to aid and assist him in the administration of the government, instead of any one of his subordinates, all of whom were expected to coöperate for the general welfare.

Mr. Lincoln was modest, kind, and unobstrusive, but he had nevertheless sturdy intellectual independence, wonderful self-reliance, and, in his unpretending way, great individuality. Though ever willing to listen to others and to avail himself of suggestions from any quarter which he deemed valuable, he never for a moment was unmindful of his position or of proper self-respect, or felt that he was "dependent" on any one for the faithful and competent discharge of any duty upon which he entered. He could have dispensed with any one of his cabinet and the administration not been impaired, but it would have been difficult if not impossible to have selected any one who could have filled the office of chief magistrate as successfully as Mr. Lincoln in that troublesome period. In administering the government, there were details in each department with which he did not interfere or attempt to make himself familiar—a routine which the Secretaries respectively discharged. Of these the President had a general knowledge, and the executive control of each and all. In this respect the Secretary of State bore the same relation to the President as his colleagues in the other departments. Mr. Lincoln well understood the nature of the differences which existed in the Republican party—the causes which had influenced the members of the Chicago Convention, and the policy which it was expected would characterize his administration. His sympathies, feelings, and views were in harmony and full accord with those who had secured his nomination; and, faithful in his convictions and to his trust, he would not permit those who selected him to be disappointed, nor allow himself to be diverted from that policy nor to organize a Cabinet opposed to it.

But the same influences which operated and were defeated at Chicago in nominating a candidate, early obtruded themselves on the President elect in attempts to control his selection of his executive council. Mr. Seward and his special friends, who still clung to the old Whig party, and hoped by some device to renew and prolong it, were apprehensive that there would be too strong an infusion of the Democratic element in the Cabinet. They did not propose to wholly exclude men of Democratic antecedents, but it was urged that the Whig element should, for the sake of harmony, and efficient, concerted, united action, have a decided preponderance. Mr. Lincoln quietly listened to these representations, but he well understood the object, and avoided the path to which they invited him. Instead of yielding to them, he was confirmed in his convictions that the Republican policy which led to his nomination and election was right, and should be maintained independent of old parties and old organizations. Discarding the importunities of the Albany mission which visited him in Springfield, he brought into his Cabinet an equal number from each of the old opposing parties, which would enable him to get the opinions of men of differing political views. It was with two exceptions the same as that with which four months later he commenced his administration. His first cast of the persons to compose the administration was as follows:

LINCOLN	JUDD
SEWARD	CHASE
BATES	BLAIR
DAYTON	WELLES

The four names in the first column, including that of Mr. Lincoln himself, were of men who in their political antecedents had been Whigs, while the four in the opposite parallel column were Democrats in their principles and convictions though Mr. Chase had never identified himself with the democratic organization. He was distinctly anti-slavery, but concurred with the democrats in supporting the rights of the states and was an advocate of a strict construction of the constitution.

Norman B. Judd of Chicago, was an active and influential politician of Illinois, and for many years a leading member of the legislature of that state. He was also a member of the Republican National Committee, and probably did more than any other one individual to bring forward and secure the nomination of Mr. Lincoln, for whom he had a high regard and friendship, which was fully reciprocated. The President informed me that he had personally a stronger desire that Judd should be associated with him in the administration than any one else but he was from Illinois, and there were political and other circumstances which intervened. Instead of a Cabinet appointment therefore, Judd received the Prussian Mission, which he filled during Mr. Lincoln's administration, but he was recalled soon after Mr. Lincoln's death, on representations made by Mr. Seward.

William L. Dayton of New Jersey, who was designated for a position in the original cast of the Cabinet was appointed Minister to France. He had been the successful competitor with Mr. Lincoln for the nomination of Vice President in 1858, and was held in especial esteem by him. There was, however, as usual a strong local claim for Pennsylvania, without any distinguished statesman in whom the President had such faith and confidence as he had in Mr. Dayton, but the pressure from without as well as from within the State, with certain complications of his friends led to the substitution of Mr. Cameron. It was the first intention of the President, as I have understood, after this substitution, to have conferred on Mr. Dayton the mission to St. James, but Mr. Seward who was to have charge of Foreign Affairs preferred and urged that Mr. Adams should have the English appointment, and Mr. Dayton, therefore, received the mission to France.

These changes in the original programme or cast of the Cabinet did not affect the purpose of the President to have in his council an equal number of men of opposite parties in the past. Caleb Smith a Whig, and Simon Cameron a democrat took the places of Judd a democrat and Dayton a whig.

But although this was his first programme he was wisely reticent, and kept his own counsel. When, however, his intentions finally became known, and the names of the gentlemen whom he proposed to call to his side were ascertained, there was an emphatic dissent on the part of the special managing friends of Mr. Seward. Two of the gentlemen were especially excepted to, as extreme Democrats, antagonistic to Mr. Seward, who had been instrumental against him, especially at Chicago, and to whom he could scarcely be reconciled in administrative duties. But objectionable as these men were, the opposition to Mr. Chase was still more decisive; and it was intimated that if these gentlemen, particularly the last referred to, were to receive Cabinet appointments, Mr. Seward might decline the association. This intimation had no effect on Mr. Lincoln, nor did it in the least change his determination. While willing to accept and desirous to have the services of Mr. Seward and the support of his friends, he did not feel that "it was absolutely indispensable on every account" to secure him above others, or to the exclusion of others, or to be governed by him and his likes or dislikes in the choice of confidants or the make-up of his political family. In point of fact, there was strong opposition among his friends to Mr. Seward's appointment. He had no apprehensions whatever that he should not be able to have Mr. Seward in his council; and if the gentlemen whom he selected had not in their party antecedents, or in certain fundamental political opinions agreed, but were now Republicans in accord with him on present questions, that was sufficient for his purpose. Old things in parties were with him done away. There was a new departure in political organizations. His administration and his Cabinet were to be Republican irrespective of past parties. But schemes to secure a Seward Cabinet commenced early, and were persistently followed up to the inauguration. Weed, as already remarked, did not return to Albany after the Chicago nomination until he visited, and had an interview with Mr. Lincoln in his "secluded abode," at Springfield, the capital of Illinois. This was the beginning, and nothing was accomplished. Late in the Summer, Weed met certain gentlemen in Saratoga, when something definite respecting the Cabinet in the event of Mr. Lincoln's election was attempted. After the election Mr. Lincoln was urged to visit Auburn and consult Mr. Seward, who "had a plurality of votes on the first ballot" at Chicago, but he declined the invitation. It was winter, the address says, "at quite a late period of the session, before he had disclosed his intention to place Mr. Seward in the most prominent place in the Cabinet."

Most of the facts in relation to the formation of the Cabinet I received from the mouth of Mr. Lincoln, who had apparently no concealments on the subject. On the day of the presidential election, November 3d, 1860, he said, the telegraph operator at Springfield invited him to occupy his room and obtain intelligence of the result as it was received. About two o'clock on Wednesday morning sufficient information had come in to leave no doubt of his election. He then retired, but hardly to sleep. Although fatigued and exhausted, he got but little rest. Oppressed with the overwhelming responsibility that was upon him, which in the excitement of the campaign he had not fully realized, he felt the necessity of relief and assistance to sustain him in the not distant future. He did, he said, what probably all his predecessors had done— looked about him at once for the men on whom he could depend, and who would be his support in the trials that were before him. The reliable and marked men of the country were in his mind, but there were many other things to be taken into consideration—different influences, sectional and political, to be reconciled. He did not again sleep until he had constructed the framework of his Cabinet. It was essentially the same as that with which four months later he commenced his administration. This voluntary and unsolicited statement was from the man whose mind, Mr. Adams says, months after his election, " had not even opened to the nature of the crisis." Circumstances and extended details which Mr. Lincoln gave, relating to individuals and movements, Cabinet and other appointments need not be here introduced. This generalization is evidence that even at that period he had a policy and purpose, which he carried into effect, wholly distinct from and independent of the plans which Mr. Seward and his friends had marked out. He preferred to select his own advisers, and did so instead of permitting Mr. Seward to do it for him. He had in view a Republican, not a Whig administration, and therefore required and formed a Republican Cabinet. There was but one member of it appointed on the special, urgent recommendation and advice of Mr. Seward and his friends, who preferred him to Mr. Chase for the Treasury, but that gentleman was soon with Mr. Seward's approval, transferred to hyperborean regions, in a way and for reasons never publicly and distinctly made known.

The unhappy condition of the country during the winter of 1861 is not overstated in the "Memorial Address." It was as well understood and as deeply deplored at Springfield and in remote sections as at Washington, where Congress frittered away its time, and pursued a course as unpatriotic as, and scarcely less reprehensible than, the Administration which proclaimed its inability to coerce a state. The President elect witnessed the factious and disunion proceedings with unutterable distress, but he was powerless; and it was among the most painful afflictions of his varied and eventful life, to know and feel that he could do nothing to arrest threatened and impending calamities. Through the weary winter months that intervened between the election in November and the inauguration in March, he beheld the executive authority paralyzed or wielded in the interest of those who threatened the integrity of the Union. Mr. Adams says:

"Treason had crept into the very heart of the Cabinet, and a policy had been secretly at work to paralyze rather than to fortify the resources of the Executive. Everything was drifting at the mercy of the wind and waves. . . . A message was sent to Congress by Mr. Buchanan lamenting the fact of what he chose to call a secession of several States, but coupling with it a denial of any power to coerce them. This was in its essence an abandonment of all right to control popular resistance in that form. In the condition things were at that moment, with a Cabinet divided and both branches of the legislature utterly without spirit to concert measures, the effect was equivalent to disintegration."

What executive or legislative energy or ability was manifested by Congress at that crisis? Mr. Lincoln was a private citizen, " at home in Illinois," while this "secession of several states" was going on, holding no office, exercising no authority, "giving no signs of life," Mr. Adams says; but well aware that every movement and every expression of his were watched and weighed not only by secessionists, but by men in place who did nothing to relieve but much to oppose and embarrass him in the duties upon which he was soon to enter. Mr. Seward was at that time in the Senate, in a position where a disinterested and patriotic statesman of experience, sagacity, and foresight, possessed of an energetic, capable, and master mind, and of executive power, would be expected to detect and expose error and make a decisive stand against avowed and approaching treason—treason which had in fact already, says the address, crept "into the very heart of the Cabinet." But there was not a measure of resistance, scarcely a note of alarm or even of apprehension, from the New York Senator, who " received a plurality of votes" for President on the first ballot in the Chicago Convention, and who was at the time not only a Senator but the accredited Secretary of State of the incoming Administration. To him, an actor in an exalted official position, a Senator of reputed sagacity and known experience, who was in daily personal and official intercourse with men of all parties, at the seat of government, the President elect from his "secluded abode," and the whole country indeed, naturally looked with some degree of expectation, if not of great confidence, for decisive action, or at least correct information as to the state of affairs and probable results. Mr. Seward had a theory, but not such as to either inspire hope or create alarm. It was of a pacific tendency, and calculated to calm apprehensions in that "perilous emergency." He anticipated, and said, there would be harmony and reconciliation within ninety days. If sincere in his prophetic assertions, he did not exhibit intelligence or statesmanship superior to Mr. Lincoln; if insincere, he was even less reliable and faithful. Mr. Lincoln had the inclination and certainly the wish to believe that his selected counsellor, who was in the Senate, with opportunities at the time superior to himself or any other man to know the facts, was correct in his predictions and conclusions. Unfortunately Mr. Seward was mistaken. Mr. Adams says: "Wiseacres have commented on his failure of sagacity in making over-confident predictions. But what was he to do in the face of all the nations of the earth?" He certainly was not to falsify the truth; he was not to sacrifice his integrity, nor did the "wiseacres" accuse him of any such sacrifice when they "commented on his failure of sagacity." It is to be presumed that he believed what he asserted, even if it makes him a less "sagacious statesman" than is represented in the "Memorial Address." His sagacity is not to be fortified at the expense of his veracity.

The truth is, Mr. Seward did not, even at that late day, realize to its full extent the nature of the impending conflict, but viewed it as a severe and embittered party controversy, not unlike others the country had experienced, and which, being really causeless, he hoped and believed time and the change of administration would pacify. Many of his associates as well as himself were of the party of expedients, and persuaded him and themselves that if once in power he could so manage as to allay dissension, prevent secession, and effect a restoration of Union feeling. Hence, without any avowed reason, nothing but past "experience," he predicted the speedy peaceful solution of a dispute or controversy that to others looked formidable, and which soon not only threatened but assailed the Union. His predictions were in harmony with the policy, so far as he had a policy, of himself and friends. He was for peace, and had faith, hope, and confidence that peace would be preserved by some expedient, device, or luck—he knew not how—and he therefore predicted it.

Mr. Lincoln was comforted by the assurances and predictions of his future minister then in the Senate, but he had apprehensions which no prophetic declarations could entirely put at rest. Results have shown that "in this perilous interval," he, "in his secluded abode in the heart of Illinois," with unpretending yet undoubted sagacity, had a more correct knowledge and better appreciation of the condition of affairs—foresaw with more accurate perception the threatened difficulties—than the experienced politicians who predicted and promised peace. Those who best knew the two men are aware that their minds were widely different inherently and in their organization. The President was greatly superior in intellectual strength and vigor, had the more solid and substantial qualities, more earnestness and sincerity, a greater grasp and comprehension, a more intuitive and far-seeing sagacity, came almost instinctively to right conclusions, had more correct convictions, greater self-reliance, greater firmness of purpose, a stricter adherence to principles which he believed to be correct; points that were best understood by those who knew him best.

The Secretary of State had, with higher culture and scholastic attainments, quickness of apprehension, wonderful facility and aptness in adapting himself to circumstances and exigencies which he could not control, and a fertility in expedients, with a dexterity in adopting or dismissing plans and projected schemes, unsurpassed; qualities which made him an acceptable companion, if not always a safe adviser, but never the superior and controlling executive mind. His training and habit were partisan, and his acts often impulsive; but, accustomed through his whole official life to consult a faithful friend, to whose judgment and guidance he deferred, he had not in great emergencies the self-reliance, energy, will, and force of character which are essential to a truly great and strong executive. He sometimes acted rashly, not always wisely. But if he had not the will which is necessary for a chief, he had the sustaining qualities which are valuable in serving a capable leader with whom he might be identified. He was subordinate to Abraham Lincoln, and deferred to him as he had deferred to Thurlow Weed

—conformed to the views of the former as he had for thirty years to those of the latter—and assumed credit in the one case as it had always been given him in the other, without being the originating and directing mind in either. After the subsidence of the anti-masonic excitement on which he was first carried into office, he became a Whig, and through all its changes and mutations, until the organization was extinguished, he "adhered to the party."

Mr. Lincoln, on the contrary, was divested of partisanship beyond almost any man in active public life; not that he was insensible to party and its claims, but they were secondary and subordinate to principles—the means rather than the end. He "drifted," as he used to say, into the Whig organization at the beginning; his associations were chiefly there, but he had no particular veneration for the party or regard for many of its professed doctrines. Time, experience, reflection, and observation weakened whatever feeling or sympathy he once entertained for mere party. Unlike Mr. Seward, he had no reluctance in giving up the Whig organization; no lingering affection for it, nor any hesitation to participate in and urge on the Republican movement from its inception. Mr. Seward was an adroit and skilful party tactician, familiar with the tricks and contrivances in which his *fidus Achates* indulged to carry an election; while Mr. Lincoln had no taste, inclination, or respect for such practices, and would not, to secure party success, intentionally, even in the most excited election, deceive or permit others to deceive those who trusted him. The minds of the two men ran in different channels, and when they came together on important questions, that of the President was the principal, and not, as represented in the address, the tributary.

Mr. Adams says:

"Mr. Lincoln could not fail soon to perceive the fact that whatever estimate he might put on his own natural judgment, he had to deal with a superior in native intellectual power, in extent of acquirement, in breadth of philosophic experience, and in the force of moral discipline. On the other hand, Mr. Seward could not have been long blind to the deficiencies of the chief in these respects, however highly he might value his integrity of purpose, his shrewd capacity, and his generous and amiable disposition.... Thus it happened that Mr. Seward voluntarily dismissed forever the noblest dreams of an ambition he had the clearest right to indulge, in exchange for a more solid power to direct affairs for the benefit of the nation, through the name of another, who should yet appear in all later time to reap the honors due chiefly to his labors."

On no consideration would I detract one iota from the just merits of the late Secretary of State, with whom, though sometimes differing, I for eight years, under two Executives, enjoyed uninterruptedly pleasant, social and official intercourse; nor am I willing to see the memory of the distinguished Chief Magistrate who served his country so faithfully and so well, and finally died in her cause, unjustly obscured, and his abilities and deeds belittled and wronged. As is elsewhere said in the address, "It is the duty of history, in dealing with all human action to do strict justice in discriminating between persons, and by no means to award to one, honors that clearly belong to another." Yet a more flagrant violation of " the duty of history" in that respect, a more erroneous and unjust discrimination, or a more unrighteous "award to one honors that clearly belong to another," is scarcely to be found in all history than in the assumption that Mr. Seward directed the affairs of the nation through the name of Mr. Lincoln. Mr. Adams omits to state in what particular Mr. Seward, aside from his own department, "exercised the more solid power to direct affairs for the benefit of the nation" of which Mr. Lincoln was "in all later time to receive the honors." It was not in the management of the finances and establishing and maintaining the credit of the Government through a wasting war. I am not aware that he ever made a suggestion, proposed a measure, or in any way attempted to interfere with, or direct the affairs of the Treasury Department. There was a personal intimacy between him and the Secretary of War, but I do not remember that he proposed or directed the conduct of a single campaign, or originated any military or army movement, save some unfortunate and irregular proceedings early in the administration, when he took upon himself, as Secretary of State, to perform secretly and improperly the duties of Secretary of War without the knowledge of that officer. On one or two occasions when he attempted, in total disregard of good government and correct administration, to intermeddle with naval matters, the proceedings were, as with the War Department, disapproved as irregular, improper, and reprehensible. In the administration and operations of the Navy Department he had no part; not a single naval expedition was undertaken on his recommendation, and the most important ones were in progress without his knowledge and far advanced before he was informed of them. In the affairs and management of the other three departments he participated no more than in those mentioned, or than did other members of the Cabinet. The conduct of foreign affairs was of course, intrusted to him under the supervision and control of the President, who directed the governmental policy, and sometimes overruled, modified, and improved the dispatches which the Secretary had with great industry prepared. Mr. Seward held a ready and prolific pen, and had a mind fertile in expedients, but his judgment and conclusions were not always so sound and reliable as to pass without revision and Executive emendations and approval. Measures and important movements of each of the departments were generally, but not always, submitted to the Cabinet. The President was invariably consulted, but the Secretary of State stood in this respect like his colleagues, and his opinion and judgment, like theirs, was taken as were the others for what, in the estimation of Mr. Lincoln, they were worth. The policy of the President and the course of administration were based on substantial principles and convictions to which he firmly adhered. Mr. Seward relied less on fixed principle than expedients, and trusted to dexterity and skill rather than the rightfulness of a cause to carry him through emergencies.

The construction of Mr. Lincoln's Cabinet was, with perhaps one exception, his own work. He would have been glad to call into his council a statesman from the South of marked ability and influence, but there were difficulties which prevented. The gentlemen whom he finally selected had no previous intimacy, personal or political, nor were there antagonisms to prevent harmony and concerted action. Between Seward and Chase there was imputed rivalry, and until within two days of the inauguration the opposition of the friends of the former to placing Mr. Chase in the Treasury was active and persistent. Each of these gentlemen had high aspirations. Each had been the chief Executive of his State. Each had represented his State in the Senate, and each had a distinct party position, and, to some extent, a personal following, which made the competition interesting. Mr. Seward was a Republican with centralizing tendencies, and had been prominent in the once powerful Whig organization which had fallen into decay. Mr. Chase was a federal Republican, favorable to State rights, not attached to, nor strictly identified with, either of the old party organizations, but had been for years a conspicuous leader in the anti-slavery movement which was rising on the ruins of the Whig party. Their colleagues, aware of these differences and rivalries, were indifferent to them, and arrayed themselves under the banners of neither. It would be invidious to attempt to institute a comparison between these two gentlemen thus situated and associated; but the "Memorial Address" of Mr. Adams places Mr. Seward in the front rank of the anti-slavery movement—a "veteran reformer"—when, in fact, he had been one of the prominent members of a very different party, which, like the Democratic organization, carefully abstained from connection with that movement, while Mr. Chase was for years a prominent anti-slavery champion—openly, boldly, and irrespective of all other parties or organizations, its active and efficient advocate. In the appointment of these two men, Mr. Lincoln, who adopted the policy of Washington in bringing men of opposing principles into his Cabinet, provided they harmonized in measures of administration, reversed the original arrangement by giving to Seward, a Republican centralist, the post of Jefferson, a State rights federal Republican, and to Chase, a federal Republican, the post which Washington assigned to Hamilton, a centralist.

Mr. Seward entered upon his duties with the impression, undoubtedly, which Mr. Adams seems to have imbibed, that he was to be *de facto* President, and, as the premier in the British Government, to "direct the affairs of the nation in the name of another." The consequences were that confusion and derangement prevailed to some extent at the commencement by reason of the mental activity, assumptions, and meddlesome intrusions of the Secretary of State in the duties and affairs of others, which were, if not disorganizing, certainly not good administration. Confidence and mutual frankness on public affairs and matters pertaining to the Government, particularly on what related to present and threatened disturbances, existed among all the members, with the exception of

Mr. Seward, who had, or affected, a certain mysterious knowledge which he was not prepared to impart. This was accepted as a probable necessity by his associates, for he had been in a position to ascertain facts which it was intimated he could not perhaps well disclose. It early became apparent, however, that the Secretary of State had ideas and notions of his own position and that of his colleagues, as well as of the character and attitude of the President, that others could not admit or recognize. Secretiveness, subtle expedients, and mysterious management, which limited the knowledge of certain important transactions to the State Department, but of which the President was in some degree and from time to time partially informed, were the initiative Albany methods of executive government. This reserve it appeared from subsequent disclosures consisted of an understanding between himself and certain leading opponents with whom he had held private conference during the winter, the main purpose of which was to prevent any collision or decisive movement during the remnant of Mr. Buchanan's administration. The motives of Mr. Seward in promoting delay, were undoubtedly well-intentioned, founded on faith that he, if in power, could in some way, by some expedient reconcile differences. The secessionists had other objects. They knew it would be more difficult to unite the southern people in a war against the Buchanan administration than against Lincoln, the " black republican " whose election they had opposed and whom they declared and caused those who confided in them to believe to be an enemy to the South. The politicians, in Congress and out of it, who gathered in and about Washington that winter were willing to postpone action during the few remaining days of the expiring administration, and none more so than the feeble and irresolute, but not unintelligent or unpatriotic President who felt himself incapable of firmly holding the reins and successfully guiding the government in that crisis. Ill-advised, bewildered, paralyzed and betrayed, he readily caught at any plan which would give him quiet, and enable him to tide over the short remnant of his official life. The private conference of the leaders during this winter led to temporary arrangements, armistices and humiliating terms with avowed disunionists, acquiescence in the seizure of forts, arsenals and other public property. The government was to do nothing to preserve the union while the rebels were active and permitted to organize and do everything to resist the national authority after the 4th of March, should the secession demands not be complied with, and exaction not be met by concession.

The failures to take prompt, energetic, and decisive measures against the secession movements at the commencement, and thus, like Andrew Jackson in 1832, to "resist the beginning of evil," displayed on the part of Mr. Buchanan great want of executive ability. The indecision of the president, and the efforts of others to put off for a few weeks the evil day, was, from whatever motive, unfortunate for the reputation of President Buchanan, but more unfortunate for the country. In every point of view the temporizing policy of the winter of 1861 may be considered a mistake, a national misfortune. Not that a war could have been prevented. The conflict which had been thirty years maturing was so deep seated, its proportions were so vast, the passions had become so excited that no earthly power could have saved the country from war. The men who combined against the government for alleged grievances had, after long preparation, finally succeeded in obtaining control of the civil organization of the states in one section of the union and were determined to have the ascendency in the general government, or a new confederacy of their own. But if hostilities could not have been prevented, it is scarcely to be doubted they would have been of less proportions had the administration of Mr. Buchanan put forth the strong hand of power against the first organization to disorganize, and protected, defended and held the fortresses and public property intrusted to its keeping. But the friends of the incoming and outgoing administrations in Washington concurred in acting on a different policy, though from different motives. The secessionists felt truly that to them delay was important, that it would be an embarrassing and unhappy, if not a disastrous complication for them to make open war on the government while it was administered by a man of their own selection and whose general course they approved. Mr. Seward who was in pretty free communication with, though politically opposed to them, persuaded himself that if the contestants did not take the field until there was a change of administration, he could then, with his fertility of resources, expedients and means, tranquillize the country. In this he was as sincere as in any political act of his life. Those who charge him with unpatriotic and ulterior designs against the government and the union, do him injustice; he was a centralist in his tendencies, not a disunionist, and in his efforts to delay action he was on what Mr. Adams calls "the delusive track of expediency," without fixed principles, or any clear and well defined policy. His prophecies of pacification within ninety days, iterated and reiterated, were based on no facts. He never made known what he proposed to do to reconcile differences except as declared in his speech of the twelfth of January, by meeting exaction with concession, submitting to the doctrine of coercion and evacuating the national fortresses in the seceding states. With faith in expedients he expressed his readiness for a national convention to revise the constitution, and also for an amendment to prohibit forever, beyond revocation, any authority in Congress to interfere with the subject of slavery. As the war was inevitable and soon came "with all its horrid cost," it was fortunate for the country that so honest, so determined, so sagacious and capable a man as Lincoln was President to meet it, with his comprehensive ability, human instincts, fixed principles, calm forbearance and regard for Federal and state rights.

For several weeks after the inauguration, no stated Cabinet meetings were held, though the members were frequently assembled in council—sometimes only a part; but whenever convened, it was by special notice from the Secretary of State. This irregular practice, initiated and pressed by the Secretary of State, who was supposed to be familiar with usage and to have great executive experience, was after some weeks corrected, and stated meetings on Tuesdays and Fridays were ordered, against the remonstrance of Secretary Seward, who thought stated meetings caused unnecessary interruptions of business, and that often only a part of the members, such as were specially interested in the subjects under consideration, need be called to meet him and the President. It is mentioned in the "Memorial Address," that "Mr. Seward himself came into the State Department with no acquaintance with the forms of business other than that obtained incidentally through his services in the Senate." This was soon obvious to the whole council, who were much annoyed for a time by this want of proper system and that correct administration which is essential to intelligent unity in the Government. Under evident misapprehension of his own powers and duties, and in disregard of what belonged to others, the Secretary of State undertook too much, found himself embarrassed by promises and assurances inconsiderately given; and with no clear and well-defined policy, but with assumption of pretty unlimited authority and faith in expedients, on which, rather than substantial principles, he relied, there were for a brief period some singular proceedings. President Lincoln bore with these things patiently, though greatly embarrassed, for the omens abroad were portentous. Incidents and occurrences which actually took place will best illustrate the condition of affairs, the men, and their relative positions in administering the government.

Within a month after the advent of Mr. Lincoln and the organization of his Cabinet, the Secretary of State exhibited his loose ideas of government, his want of system and defect of correct executive and administrative talent by preparing and sending out an irregular military expedition for the relief of Fort Pickens, without consulting the Secretary of War and without his knowledge or that of any of his associates. There is not in the archives and history of the Government a record of such mischievous maladministration, when all the circumstances are considered, as this secret scheme of the Secretary of State to send, without consulting the War Department or the General-in-Chief, a military expedition to Pickens, which had already been relieved. Military and naval appropriations were not at his disposal, but he assumed their expenditure. Officers and men of both the War and Navy Departments were surreptitiously, and without the knowledge of either the Secretary of War or Secretary of the Navy, withdrawn from legitimate duty; the funds and means provided for their respective departments by Congress, and legally under their control, for which they, and not the Secretary of State, were responsible, and which were destined by them and the government for different objects, were secretly abstracted and diverted to purposes of which neither of them, nor any member of the Cabinet, was informed. In consequence of this strange misgovernment there was confusion, disorganization, and demoralization; the records of the War and Navy Departments were made unreliable and apparently false; officers were away from their assigned duty; funds were misapplied; important movements were paralyzed and defeated; the course of the Administration was interrupted and incomprehensible, and it is not surprising that it was accused of weakness and mismanagement. No satisfactory solution was ever made or attempted for these erratic and intrusive proceedings, other than rumors or charges that the Secretary of State had given assurances in regard to Fort Sumter that were unauthorized, and which could in no other way be carried out.

The condition of Fort Sumter and the necessity of measures for its relief were the first matters pressed upon the President, even before his Cabinet was organized. In his Inaugural Address he had said, " The power confided to me will be used to hold, occupy, and possess the property and places belonging to the Government." This was his policy; but the Secretary of State, who had different views, opposed sending reinforcements to Sumter, and in his opposition he was sustained by General Scott, to whom the subject was first properly referred as a military question. General Scott gave his "hearty coöperation," to Mr. Seward, and reported against sending supplies. All the Cabinet, except Mr. Blair, acquiesced in the military recommendation; but the President, after repeated discussions, rejected the advice of Mr. Seward and adhered to his own original policy. The decision was a great disappointment to the Secretary of State. It was subsequently alleged, and has never been denied, that he had promised the rebels that Sumter should be evacuated. Thurlow Weed admitted in the Albany Evening Journal that such a promise had been made, but though Mr. Weed appears to have been informed of the fact, the Cabinet was not. The President was not a party to any such assurance, knew not of it, and never gave it his sanction. Here, at the very commencement of the Administration, the two minds were in direct antagonism on a subject of momentous national interest. The president, who is represented as "having been selected partly on account of the absence of positive qualities," with a "mind not opened to the nature of the crisis," as subordinate and deficient in "native intellectual power," had a policy of his own in which he persisted, though opposed by the Secretary of State, aided by the General-in-Chief and the acquiescence of all but one of the Cabinet. His countrymen were with him and his views, not with the Secretary of State.

One evening in the latter part of the month of March there was a small gathering at the Executive Mansion while the Sumter question was still pending. The members of the Cabinet were soon individually and quietly invited to the council-chamber, where, as soon as assembled, the President informed them he had just been advised by General Scott that it was expedient to evacuate Fort Pickens as well as Fort Sumter, which last was assumed at military headquarters to be a determined fact in conformity with the views of Secretary Seward and the General-in-Chief. This astounding announcement was the more surprising from the fact that the Navy Department had, about a fortnight previously, on the 12th of March, on the special application of General Scott, sent the steamer Mohawk to the squadron off Pensacola with orders to land Captain Vogdes and his command, and thus reinforce Pickens. No word had been received from the fort, or from any quarter, that rendered necessary or even expedient this unaccountable change of military operations. A brief silence followed the announcement of the amazing recommendation of General Scott, when Mr. Blair, who had been much annoyed by the vacillating course of the General-in-Chief in regard to Sumter, remarked, looking earnestly at Mr. Seward, that it was evident the old general was playing politician in regard to both Sumter and Pickens; for it was not possible, if there was a defence, for the rebels to take Pickens; and the Administration would not be justified if it listened to his advice and evacuated either. Very soon thereafter, I think at the next Cabinet meeting, the President announced his decision that supplies should be sent to Sumter, and issued confidential orders to that effect. All were gratified with this decision except Mr. Seward, who still remonstrated, but preparations were immediately commenced to fit out an expedition to forward supplies. To the surprise of the Administration, information of the confidential order to reinforce Sumter was promptly sent to Charleston. It was subsequently ascertained that this telegram was sent by Mr. Harvey, a newspaper correspondent, who was intimate at the State Department. Mr. Harvey himself was soon after appointed Minister to Portugal, on the recommendation and by request of Mr. Seward.

It was on the twenty-eighth of March that the President informed the Cabinet of his determination to relieve the garrison in Fort Sumter. On the following day, the twenty-ninth of March, Mr. Seward instituted his secret military expedition, without consulting the Secretary of War or General Scott. Until this time there had been "hearty coöperation" between them, but on the twenty-ninth Mr. Seward took Montgomery C. Meigs, then a captain of engineers, to the President, saying, " he thought the President ought to see some of the younger officers, and not consult only with men who, if the war broke out, could not mount a horse," as General Scott could not. The General had from some cause or influence during the winter abandoned his original Jacksonian recommendation to President Buchanan that the forts in the South should be occupied and strengthened. He now advised President Lincoln to a different policy, and that Sumter and Pickens should be evacuated. Two days before the inauguration he had so far yielded to the secession movement as to propose in a private letter to Mr. Seward as a last alternative, to permit "the wayward sisters to go in peace."

This letter of the second of March was addressed to Mr. Seward who does not appear to have dissented from it. On the contrary, knowing the position of General Scott, consulting and advising with him through the winter, aware of, if he was not instrumental in, inducing the General to change his original recommendation to President Buchanan that the forts at the South ought to be garrisoned and strengthened, Mr. Seward, when the question of reinforcing Fort Sumter was under consideration advised that the whole subject should be referred to General Scott and that his report should be conclusive. At the time he so advised, Mr. Seward was aware of the altered views or position of General Scott, but no other member of the Cabinet was informed of the fact. On the eleventh of March, General Scott made special personal and urgent application for a naval vessel to convey an officer who would be a bearer of dispatches with instructions to Captain Vogdes on the steamer Brooklyn off the harbor of Pensacola to disembark his men and reinforce Fort Pickens. After orders had gone forward to New York to receive and convey this officer, I, on the evening of the succeeding day, the twelfth, received a note from the general stating he would not send an officer but a written order which would be sufficient. The earnest zeal of the preceding day had, from some cause for which I could not account, abated; the change in that emergency for which he gave no reason struck me with surprise, nevertheless I sent directions for Commander Strong of the Mohawk to carry and deliver the dispatch, if Commander Craven of the Crusader had sailed.

Not until the President, a fortnight later made known to the Cabinet the recommendation of General Scott to evacuate Pickens as well as Sumter, and I heard the remark from Mr. Blair that he was playing politician instead of general could I account for the change from the programme of the twelfth.

The unanimous rejection of his proposition to evacute Pickens, and the decision to reinforce Sumter, weakened the influence of General Scott and changed Mr. Seward's tactics. Captain Meigs was substituted as military adviser of the Secretary of State and manager of details in his secret military operations. This method of taking subordinates into the confidence of the Secretary of State, ignoring the whole Cabinet, and of administering the different departments of the government, was never before practised, and will at no time bear very close inspection. General Scott, who had primarily confided implicitly in Mr. Seward was more surprised than any other, at the course things had taken.

The President, in the legitimate discharge of his functions as the chief executive officer of the government, directed that supplies should be sent to Sumter, and his confidential executive orders to that effect became an absorbing administration measure. Military preparations were made, and a squadron was promptly fitted out by the Navy Department within one week from the date of the executive order to coöperate with the military, and instructions, sanctioned and approved by the President, were given to Captain Mercer, of the steam frigate Powhatan, to command the squadron and proceed off Charleston harbor. The other vessels were directed to report to him on the 11th of April ten miles due east from Charleston lighthouse. But the whole plan and arrangement were defeated. Not only were the rebels advised of the confidential movements of the Administration by Harvey, and Governor Pickens by particular request of Mr. Seward informed of the intentions of the President to send supplies but not troops, if the supplies were peaceably received; but at the moment of sailing the expedition was deprived of its commander and flagship. Captain Mercer was displaced from the command without the knowledge of the Secretary of the Navy and the entire squadron, when it arrived at the place of rendezvous, was destitute of a naval commander, flagship, and instructions. The Powhatan, with boats, supplies, and men destined for Sumter, had been withdrawn from the service to which she was especially ordered, and sent, without naval orders or record, under a different and junior commander, on a secret and useless mission to Pensacola, by the Secretary of State. None of these orders emanated from, passed through, or were known to the Navy or War Departments. The whole proceeding, in all its parts, was irregular, disorganizing, bad administration, and deficient in executive ability. The President, who, without giving the subject much consideration, had assented to the scheme of the Secretary of State to reinforce Pickens, was not aware that the flagship of the squadron to Charleston had been detached, and its commander superseded, until the evening of the 6th of April, on which day the Powhatan sailed under a different officer for a distant destination, carrying off supplies, munitions, and boats which the Navy Department had ordered for Sumter. I was not made acquainted with this secret proceeding until the Powhatan sailed, when I immediately informed the President. So soon as aware of the fact, he directed Mr. Seward, although it was then midnight, to telegraph forthwith and countermand the orders which detached that vessel; to reinstate Mercer, and in no way to interfere with the arrangements of the Secretary of the Navy. Mr. Seward remonstrated, claimed that the Powhatan was essential to reinforce Pickens, but the President was decided. A brief and curious telegram was sent by Mr. Seward in his own name to New York, and a fast boat despatched from the Navy Yard which overtook the Powhatan at Staten Island, but nothing was accomplished. The Sumter expedition sailed without a naval commander, the squadron had no head, and the Powhatan, one of the three naval vessels on the Atlantic coast on which the government relied in that "perilous emergency," with her large crew and armament, was sent to the Gulf, where she was not wanted, and where almost the whole home squadron was concentrated, while the whole maritime frontier north of Cape Florida was left destitute. It was on the night of the 6th of April that the Powhatan sailed for Pickens. On the next day Mr. Seward sent to Judge Campbell, a leading secessionist on the Supreme bench: "Faith as to Sumter fully kept. Wait and see."

In these proceedings the administration and executive management of the President and Secretary of State, respectively, may be seen. The merits, sincerity, acts, and policy of each are disclosed, and from them a more correct estimate may be formed of their ability, respective fitness, and peculiar qualities to discharge the duties of chief magistrate, than from the partial and prejudiced assertions of interested partisans.

I have made mention of only certain general measures of administration in regard to the relief of Sumter, but it may be said in passing that there is an unwritten history of the transaction—of vacillating changes on the part of General Scott; of the singular notice of Major Anderson to Mr. Buchanan on the morning of the 4th of March, an hour or two before the inauguration of Mr. Lincoln and of the stirring tidings to Mr. Lincoln on his taking the inaugural oath, of the preparations and non-preparations for defence, and other planning—which is yet to be analyzed and developed, but would be inappropriate in this place.

The following letter from ex-Postmaster-General Blair, one of the surviving members of the first Cabinet of Mr. Lincoln, corroborative of the foregoing statement, and illustrative of the character and course of the late Secretary of State in other respects will be read with interest:

"Washington, May 17, 1873.

"My Dear Mr. Welles: I duly received yours of the 14th. You will have seen ere this that I have anticipated your advice and made a statement in reply to Mr. Adams on the relations of Messrs. Lincoln and Seward. I know that a fuller statement would be read with interest, but I prefer to leave that to you. I am tempted, however, to contribute a short chapter to your exposition, and to illustrate Mr. Seward's character by giving an account of his intrigue to surrender the forts and allow secession to take its course, and his sudden change of policy when he found that Mr. Lincoln would resist secession.

General Scott was his great card at the outset. Lincoln, having been a Whig and a supporter of Scott for the Presidency, had persuaded himself in the canvass that the old general was a great military man; and the general being really patriotic, and having learned from General Jackson how to deal with secession, would have given good advice, if, unfortunately, he had not fallen into Mr. Adams' error in regarding Mr. Seward as the head of the government, and for this reason surrendered his own better judgment to that of Mr. Seward. This is shown by the fact that he had advised Mr. Buchanan to reinforce the forts. But in deference to Mr. Seward he changed all this, gave up his own opinions, and said, "Let the wayward sisters go in peace;" and actually advised the surrender of Fort Pickens at Pensacola as well as Fort Sumter at Charleston!

I never shall forget the President's excitement when, after a Cabinet dinner at the White House, he called the Cabinet into a separate room, and informed us that General Scott had told him *it would be necessary to evacuate Fort Pickens as well as Fort Sumter.* It was while the question of the surrender of Fort Sumter was undecided; but at a time when it was believed the fort would be surrendered, and after the way had been prepared for it by statements in the Press that the fort was untenable. A very oppressive silence succeeded the President's statement of what General Scott had said. At length it was said this advice of the general's was enough of itself to show that he was playing politician and not general as respects Fort Sumter, as well as with respect to Fort Pickens, for there was no reason to believe that Fort Pickens could be taken from us."

"Mr. Seward had overshot the mark this time. The Cabinet generally had been convinced that Fort Sumter was untenable, and acquiesced in its surrender, submitting to the inevitable. But there was no apprehension felt about Fort Pickens. The fort was well supplied, and was actually impregnable while we commanded the sea, and we then had a large naval force there. Hence, when the general said we must give up this fort too, the President's confidence in him was staggered, and from that moment I have always thought his power with the President waned.

"When Mr. Seward saw that his policy of meeting "exaction with concession" and "violence with peace," announced in his speech of January 12, 1861, had failed, and that the President would not agree to surrender the forts, as Mr. Seward had induced General Scott to recommend him to do, he immediately telegraphed Governor Pickens, by the hands of Mr. Harvey, his Portuguese minister, that an attempt was to be made to reinforce Sumter. General Anderson had made no preparations to defend it, but left his barracks standing, to be fired at the first shot, instead of pulling them down and taking to his casemates, as he certainly would have done if he had not been *authoritatively told that the fort was to be evacuated as soon as the small supply of provisions on hand had been consumed.* But for this negligence *for which he was never chided*, the fort was impregnable, as events proved, for we could never take it from the Confederates. To make sure of defeating the relief, however, the Powhatan, on whose seamen and guns the success of this expedition wholly depended, was secretly detached, by an order surreptitiously obtained from the President, on the pretext of relieving Fort Pickens, which was in no danger, for the defence of which ample provision had already been made, and to whose relief the Powhatan was wholly unnecessary and in no way contributed.

" Mr. Seward had two objects in detaching this vessel: 1st, It defeated the relief of Fort Sumter, which he was pledged to surrender, and the failure to relieve it would vindicate his judgment in advising against the attempt. 2d, Fort Pickens could be claimed as having been saved by an expedition conceived and carried into execution under his orders, and so, though he would by this movement abandon his method of meeting " exaction with concession" and "violence with peace," he would signalize his abandonment of his peace policy by such a success in administering the force policy, as to put himself *per saltum* at the head of his opponents, discomfited by the failure of their attempt at resistance. And accordingly, though the Powhatan did but sail to Pensacola and back again, it was heralded as a great achievement.

"The result of this scheming was sad indeed. Our flag on Fort Sumter held Beauregard at Charleston. When it fell he marched into Virginia and precipitated secession there. If we could have held Fort Sumter there never would have been a drop of blood shed. It was the coercion of Virginia into the Confederacy by Beauregard's army that made the war. General Jackson held nullification in check, and compelled the repeal of the South Carolina ordinance, simply by sending Scott, with one thousand men, to hold Fort Moultrie. Sumter was infinitely stronger, and the North was relatively as much stronger than the South in 1860 as Sumter was stronger than Moultrie in 1833. Fortunately, the country was not cursed in Jackson's day with a meddling Secretary of State, to invite secession by agreeing to yield to its exactions and disarm the force ordered for its suppression, which was all-sufficient for the purpose at the start—using, without stint, his patronage and power to palm off through the Press the blundering intrigues which brought on a disastrous war, as statesmanship, and holding on to place by abandoning any policy which stood in the way of it, or by adopting any which might be required to retain it. I may misjudge Mr. Seward, but if I do it is not because I have ever had the least unkind feeling toward him personally. He never gave me the slightest reason for personal ill-will to him. My opposition to him has always been political, and because I regarded him as a most unsafe public man. He was a kindly man in his social relations, and when I met him in his home and family I enjoyed his society and was interested in him and them, and had a warm and sympathetic feeling for all that pertained to his domestic life. In that sphere I think he was a good and pure man. There was a freshness and heartiness in his manner, and his conversation so abounded in humor, and there was such an endless flow in his spirits, that I always found his society attractive. It was only against the political man that my nature revolted. He was to me the personification of old Polonius' politician, who "by indirection found direction out." Nor is this version of his character the result merely of my own observation of his conduct, or derived from the reports of others who have been associated with him. I have seen much of him, and much of those who have associated long with him. But the familiar facts of his life, derived from these sources, accord exactly with the political philosophy I have heard him propound over and over again. No one has ever associated long with him who has not heard him recount by the hour his successful political strategy. I could fill a volume with his narratives of the tricks he has played, if I could recall the half part of what I have heard from him. He really thought that politics was but a game. I shall never forget how shocked I was at his telling me that he was the man who put Archy Dixon, the Whig Senator from Kentucky in 1854, up to moving the repeal of the Missouri Compromise, as an amendment to Douglas's first Kansas bill, and had himself forced the repeal by that movement, and had thus brought to life the Republican party. Dixon was to out-herod Herod at the South, and he would out-herod Herod at the North. He did not contemplate what followed. He did not believe in the reality of the passions he excited, because he felt none himself. He thought it all a harmless game for power.

"Yours truly,
"MONTGOMERY BLAIR."

THE crowded incidents of the early days of Mr. Lincoln's Presidency, while the members of the Cabinet were new to each other, and their relative standing and authority apparently unsettled, the character of the Administration not yet defined, and the government and country much demoralized, are deeply interesting, and some of them of a singular description. In his confiding nature the President doubtless trusted much to the Secretary of State.

On the evening of the 1st of April, Mr. Nicolay, the private secretary of the President, brought me a package containing papers, instructions, and executive orders of a most extraordinary character. One of them directed me to detach Commodore Stringham, a patriotic officer whom I had called to special duty in the Navy Department, where he was employed in confidential trusts, and send him to Pensacola. Commodore Pendergrast, who had just arrived at Hampton Roads from the West Indies with the Cumberland, was ordered to repair forthwith to Vera Cruz on account of alleged complications. Why these two officers in whom I confided were selected to be sent away was a mystery. On the Cumberland and the Powhatan the Navy Department was relying to co-operate with the military, for the protection of the Navy Yard at Norfolk in case of difficulty. All these orders relating to the navy were issued by the Secretary of State without consultation with the Secretary of the Navy or any Cabinet consultation whatever. But the most extraordinary and irregular if not illegal order in that remarkable package directed a reorganization of the Navy Department, and the establishment of a new bureau, in which I was commanded to place in the most confidential relations, where he should have knowledge of all the important transactions of the navy and Navy Department, and the government, Samuel Barron, a finished courtier and shrewd secessionist. On looking over these documents it was evident to me that the President had been the victim of misplaced confidence and was sadly imposed upon, or that he was as unfit for the office of Chief Executive as is represented in the "Memorial Address." I lost not a moment in waiting upon him, and reading to him these extraordinary papers. He promptly and emphatically disavowed them; said he had hurriedly and without examination signed a large number of papers which had been brought to him by Secretary Seward for a very different purpose, and which he had supposed were merely formal; that he was not aware of their contents; had trusted entirely to Mr. Seward; and whom could he trust if not the Secretary of State? He requested me to return him the orders or treat them as nullities. The result was, no new bureau was organized without law; Barron was not taken into the confidence of the Navy Department, but soon deserted and was the first naval officer captured in the rebel service; Stringham never went to Pensacola nor Pendergrast again to Vera Cruz, nor was there any complication that required it.

It is stated that President Lincoln was "quite deficient in his acquaintance with the character and qualities of public men, or their aptitude for the positions to which he assigned them. Indeed, he never selected them solely by that standard." The authority for this statement is not given. It relates, apparently, chiefly to appointments abroad, and these appointments for which the President is held responsible, were most of them made on the recommendation of Mr. Seward, to whose department they properly appertained, and who was vigilant and tenacious in dispensing the patronage of the State Department, often without consulting others.

On this point of selecting officials, or being consulted in regard to appointments which came within the purview of his department, no man was more sensitive than Mr. Seward, though himself not always regardful of what in this respect was due to others.

In March 1861, while the Senate was in extra session, differences existed between the Secretary of State and the Senators from New York relative to the local appointments in that state. These differences resulted in a conference at the State Department, to which the President was specially invited, and consented with some reluctance to be present. It was an evening consultation, and he thought proper to invite me to accompany him. The President, Secretary

Seward, and Senators King and Harris were the only persons besides myself in attendance. Before taking up the list of names the President said he would relieve them of any difference in regard to the most important office, that of Collector, by appointing on his own responsibility and from personal knowledge, Hiram Barney, who had his confidence and was a man of integrity. There was but a single civil appointment, that of Navy Agent, connected with the Navy Department to be made. No disagreement existed concerning that, which was soon disposed of, when Mr. Seward remarked it would be unnecessary to detain me longer, but the President and the Senators desired me to remain. It is not necessary to go into the particulars of that conference, which seemed to cover most of the important appointments in the city and State of New York. After listening to the disposition of some collectorships and other offices in which there was an approximation to agreement, an intimation was thrown out by Mr. Seward that he wished the list which he had made out, and which was somewhat extended, might be completed and the nominations sent forthwith to the Senate. This embarrassed the two Senators who were unprepared for so hasty a movement. I inquired if the Secretary of the Treasury and Attorney General had been consulted, and concurred in the selection. Mr. Seward said they had not; that it was unnecessary; that these were New York appointments, and he and the Senators knew better than any others what was best for the party and the administration in that state. I remarked that Cabinet officers were responsible for the proper administration of their respective departments; that subordinates should have their confidence, and if changes were to be made of the incumbents, the new selections should be by them or with their concurrence; that to fill the offices under them with untried men whom they did not know, and without their knowledge, appeared to me improper and would be likely to cause difficulties. Mr. Seward dissented, and claimed that he knew what was best for the Administration in New York; that there were personal and party matters to be considered, which neither Mr. Chase nor Mr. Bates could understand so well as himself. I disclaimed any intention to meddle with New York parties or New York controversies; but besides courtesies which it would be well always to observe, I insisted as a sound principle and correct rule of action that the heads of departments should, if they did not select, at least be consulted in regard to the appointments of their subordinates. The President said I was right; that to fill the New York appointments as Mr. Seward wished, without consulting the Secretary of the Treasury, and others directly interested, would, he was convinced, not be satisfactory. He was willing to hear any remarks or suggestions relative to candidates, to take their recommendations; but it must be distinctly understood that there would be nothing conclusive until he advised with the heads of the departments interested. With this, the meeting soon and somewhat abruptly terminated.

Mr. Thurlow Weed has related and published more than once what he deems a creditable proceeding, which exemplifies the Albany practice of making appointments, and the method of discharging the executive functions with which he was familiar. He was going, he says, on a brief errand to Washington early in the administration, when he was requested by some of his party intimates to get a snug place for a naturalized Englishman who had for years been a willing runner, or whipper-in, for the Whigs of New York city, a sort of "Tim Linkenwater" Weed says, but who now wished to go home and spend his last days in a comfortable place in England. The request was cheerfully assented to, and Mr. Weed on the morning of his arrival, while at breakfast with the Secretary of State, communicated the wishes of their party friends, and was assured the solicited appointment should be made. Immediately, without inquiry or investigation, and while they were at breakfast, the Secretary, with his accustomed promptness, ordered the removal of the consul at Falmouth and the appointment of the party instrument "Tim Linkenwater" in his place. When Weed called at the State Department for the commission, Mr. Hunter, the old chief clerk, on delivering the document expressed his regret at the change. The consul whom you remove, said Mr. Hunter, is one of the most correct and efficient officers in the consular service, as was his father before him. That father was the open, steadfast, and true friend of our country in the war of independence. General Washington when President, in grateful remembrance of the sympathy and friendship of this English gentleman, appointed him consul at Falmouth; and on his death, General Jackson appointed the son, whom you now remove without fault or complaint after years of faithful service. It makes me sad, said the old clerk. Weed acknowledged he was ashamed. His sensibilities were touched for the man; there had been no thought for the faithful incumbent or the welfare of the government. He declined to take the commission, and the removed consul was by Mr. Weed, not by Mr. Seward, reinstated without ever knowing he had been displaced. No Secretary of State had ever before permitted a partisan editor to enter the State Department and take such freedom with important appointments. Mr. Weed assumes and is entitled to the credit of not finally consummating a wrong after he learned the facts, though he did not inquire into the case, nor did the State Department before ordering the removal.

The "Memorial Address" declares that "no experiment so rash has ever been made as that of elevating to the head of affairs a man with so little previous preparation for his task as Mr. Lincoln. If this be true of him in regard to the course of domestic administration, with which he might be supposed partially familiar, it is eminently so in respect to the foreign relations of which he knew absolutely nothing."

No greater mistake or misrepresentation could be made. Men vastly inferior to Mr. Lincoln, less qualified and less able, have been elected President; and his general knowledge of our "foreign relations," if not as minute in routine and current details as that of members of the Committee on Foreign Relations, was more enlarged and comprehensive than that of many in those positions. Some of our countrymen, who live and die in retirement without ever holding office, give attention to those subjects, and are more capable of discharging the duties, and would represent the government abroad with more ability than the persons selected. Without specifying particulars on these matters, I may mention that this man, who is represented as so totally ignorant and unfit, and so destitute of experience, and who it is said "absolutely knew nothing"—concerning them, showed intelligence, sound judgment, and correct views at the very commencement of the administration, on a most interesting occasion, above the Secretary of State, who was, by the standard of Mr. Adams, greatly his superior. In an important dispatch of the Secretary of State to Mr. Adams, who was then our Minister at London, Mr. Lincoln took the document, which he considered in some respects exceptional, criticised, modified, and with his own hand expurgated, corrected, and improved it, and changed its character. This paper related to the recognition of belligerent rights, was addressed to Mr. Adams, and is probably now on the files of the State Department in its original form, with the corrections and improvements of the President. Mr. Adams was doubtless unaware that the President, who, he says, "absolutely knew nothing" of our foreign relations, was substantially the author of the instructions to himself, and laid down the chart by which he was to be guided in a most important matter of national concernment. The President overruled and set aside some of the elaborate and important, but in his view, objectionable portions of the dispatch of Mr. Seward.

These facts are known beyond the Cabinet circle, and are consequently no secret. There were other marked cases of intelligent supervision of our foreign affairs and their management by the President in the final summing up on important questions, which overthrow the statements of Mr. Adams, who has an utterly false conception of the relative position, ability, and character of the two men of whom he speaks. To the Secretary of State, whose special duty it was to investigate and report upon international subjects, and prepare instructions to the respresentatives of the government abroad, the President gave the same, perhaps closer attention than to the Secretary of the Navy, who issued instructions and orders to the commanders of squadrons and officers on special duty. In no respect was the Secretary of State on a different footing in administering the government from other heads of departments nor did he infuse more vigor or character in the administration. He was more constant and unwearied than others in his attention to and attendance upon the President, made it a point to always accompany him in his visits to the army or wherever he appeared in public, and was personally very devoted to him, but never exercised higher executive authority or had "the more solid power to direct affairs for the benefit of the nation" than his associates. There were in the foreign policy of the government during Mr. Lincoln's administration fewer and less perplexing questions, less serious complications than under several of our previous Presidents. But the domestic administration from the commencement to its close was one of unprecedented labor and responsibility requiring energy, vigilance, executive and administrative ability, such as had never before devolved on the Chief Magistrate or the government. The action and responsibility of others were far greater than those devolved on the Secretary of State.

It is admitted by Mr. Adams that, while wanting in the qualities of President, and while "no experiment so rash has ever been made as that of elevating to the head of affairs a man with so little previous preparation for his task as Mr. Lincoln," "he afterwards proved himself before the world, a pure, brave, honest man, faithful to his arduous work." Nothing more. It is still left to be inferred that though he meant well, he was incompetent and without ability to discharge the duties of his position, except under the direction of one of his subordinates who had really less to do than others in the domestic administration of the government. It does not occur to Mr. Adams that he under estimated the ability of the President of whom he personally knew little, and that the people formed a more correct estimate of their Chief Majestrate's capacity than himself. He gives no credit to President Lincoln for far-seeing sagacity, in which he excelled most men of his time; for knowledge of the structure of the government and information on public affairs, which he had studied with diligence and passionate fondness; for arduous and successful labors, though holding no office, endowed with no wealth, and aided by no metropolitan funds, in his great struggle for constitutional freedom; for executive and administrative ability, for sound judgment, intellectual capacity, mental power, and practical knowledge, which enabled him to stand at the helm and guide the government through storms and dangers such as no country ever experienced. In all these qualities the impression is conveyed that this remarkable man was deficient, but that they were possessed by the Secretary of State, who was "not blind to the deficiencies of his chief." Indeed, the whole language, tone, tenor, sentiment, and intent of the address are to elevate Mr. Seward and depreciate Mr. Lincoln; to award to the Secretary honors that clearly belong to the President; to make it appear that the subordinate controlled and directed the principal; that the Secretary of State was *de facto* President, and the President himself a mere *locum tenens*, incompetent for the place from the want of "experience" and "previous preparation." Mr. Seward had influence in the administration, but not control. His mental activity, the "marvellous fertility of his pen," his proneness to exercise authority and to make himself conspicuous on every important subject and occasion, imposed on admiring and willing friends, who, like Mr. Adams, persuaded themselves that one so active and prominent must be the moving and directing spirit of the administration. It would be difficult, however, for his most partial friends to specify any financial, military, naval, territorial or general measure of administration, which had its origin with or was directed by the Secretary of State, while the President suggested some and directed all. Mr. Seward could adapt himself to, or adopt and appropriate the views of, others with wonderful facility and address could second their propositions, and support them with a zeal and earnestness which made them seem his own.

Mr. Adams says he knows that in order to cut up by the roots the possibility of misunderstanding or rivalry between the President and Secretary of State, "Mr. Seward deliberately came to the conclusion to stifle every sensation left him of aspiration in the future, by establishing a distinct understanding with the President on that subject." "Thus it happened that Mr. Seward voluntarily dismissed forever the noblest dreams of an ambition he had the clearest right to indulge, in exchange for a more solid power to direct affairs for the benefit of the nation through the name of another, who should yet appear in all later time to reap the honors due chiefly to his labors."

That Mr. Seward signified to the President he should not be a competitor with him for the office of Chief Magistrate in 1864 is not improbable, and but for the disparagement so ungenerously as well as unjustly thrown upon the President, who according to the "Memorial Address" was "in all later times to reap the honors due chiefly to Mr. Seward's labors," the latter should have the unrestricted credit of patriotic self-abnegation. But the truth must not be suppressed or perverted, and there are, aside from the act of declination but connected with it, certain facts and circumstances which are essential to a right understanding of the case, and which, if the subject be alluded to, truth requires should not be omitted.

In December 1862, the dissatisfaction which existed in Congress and the country against the imputed meddlesome interference and alleged mismanagement of the Secretary of State, and his supposed influence over the Executive, was such that a very general desire was expressed that he should leave the Cabinet and retire from the Administration. To some extent he had unwittingly and unintentionally contributed to the prevailing discontent by persistent and ostentatious exhibition of himself in public with the President when he visited the army, and indeed on every possible occasion, outside of the State Department. His *claqueurs* and supporters busied themselves in representing that Mr. Seward was *de facto* President, and the "Memorial Address" falls into the same error by declaring he was directing affairs. Mr. Seward gave encouragement to these representations. They gratified his vanity and that of his supporters, but did not strengthen and fortify him in Congress or with the public, as he and his friends anticipated would be the case, but really weakened him, and for a time were harmful to the President, towards whom the country was otherwise well inclined. Military reverses always weaken an administration. The people, however, are tolerant of the mistakes of their Chief Magistrate, and forbearing towards his honest errors, but are exacting and often intolerant towards subordinate or reputed favorites. Under national reverses they were lenient towards the President, and whatever was wrong they charged, sometimes improperly, on the secretaries, particularly the one who assumed the "more solid power to direct affairs," and whom they held accountable, not entirely without reason, for certain executive indiscretions and for national misfortunes.

When Congress convened in December, the sentiment or prejudice against Mr. Seward was deep and severe, but he seemed not cognizant of it, nor was the President himself aware of its full extent. He could not have been wholly ignorant of the fact that there was a growing dislike of Mr. Seward and that he was opposed by many friends of the administration as well as opponents; but he knew that others of the Cabinet were improperly censured and abused, and that he as well as they were in some cases unjustly assailed. No one, however, had warned either of the extreme disfavor with which almost the whole community in those days viewed Mr. Seward—their want of confidence in his sincerity and judgment, and their belief that his intimacy and influence with the President were pernicious. This erroneous, or, more properly speaking, exaggerated impression of the influence and power of the Secretary of State which the partisans of Mr. Seward had inculcated, in the mistaken belief that it would increase his strength to the same extent that it injured the President—a mistake into which Mr. Adams appears to have fallen—carried with it the idea that the President permitted himself to be persuaded and misled by his subordinate to do acts against his own better judgment. The assiduous attentions of the Secretary of State could scarcely fail to have some effect on the President, especially in minor matters, to which he could not always, in the overwhelming multiplicity of affairs, give that minute attention which he wished. Intimacy, companionship would unavoidably carry with it more or less influence, and in that view the Secretary had influence which he was forward to exhibit and not reluctant to exercise, sometimes unfortunately for the President and the country. It was notorious that the partisan friends of Mr. Seward were anxious to have it believed he was the power behind the President who controlled the action of the government, and some of his own oracular sayings and doings tended to that belief.

A brief interchange of views among the members after Congress assembled led to the disclosure of great unanimity of opinion adverse to the Secretary of State, which resulted in a meeting of the Republican Senators on the 17th of December, at which, resolutions in opposition to him and requesting that he should be dismissed, were adopted with but one dissenting voice. A committee of nine Senators, embracing some of the ablest and most eminent men of that body, at the head of which was the venerable Judge Collamer of Vermont, chairman of the Judiciary Committee, was appointed, and instructed to wait upon the President and communicate to him the general conviction that the continuance of Mr. Seward in office would be injurious to the administration and the country, and to make known to him a request on the part of the Senators assembled that the services of Mr. Seward should be dispensed with.

These extraordinary proceedings were immediately communicated to Secretary Seward, before the committee had waited upon the President, by Senator

King of New York, the only gentleman who had opposed them. Mr. Seward promptly and properly tendered his resignation. It is not essential to enter into the details of that movement further than to say that Mr. Lincoln defeated it, and in doing so, demonstrated to Senators and Cabinet executive ability, tact, and power such as Mr. Adams never knew he possessed, and consequently fails to appreciate. Although surprised and grieved by what was done and what he learned, the President did not submit to Senatorial dictation, nor permit the Executive Department of the government to be overborne or invaded. Mr. Seward was not dismissed, nor was his resignation accepted, nor did he wish it to be accepted. The attempt to drive him from the State Department really strengthened him in the position, but there is no doubt the movement had in some respects a beneficial effect in restraining his officiousness and in arousing Mr. Lincoln's attention to it. The scheming party management, which had been defeated first at Chicago and subsequently in the formation of the Cabinet, but which had adroitly undertaken to control and regulate the Administration, was by these Senatorial proceedings rebuked and again defeated. Some of the active Congressional friends who had favored the nomination of Mr. Seward at Chicago had become dissatisfied with him and his demonstrations, and were most forward in asking that he should not be permitted to longer discharge the duties of Secretary of State.

It was at this juncture, when he became conscious that he had no longer a party to sustain him—when he saw all the Senate, and it may be added, about the whole of the representative body opposed to him—when there was not a single state, nor any party in any state, in his favor—that "Mr. Seward deliberately came to the conclusion to stifle every sensation left in him of aspiration in the future," and "dismiss forever the noblest dreams of ambition," not that he might be or was thereby able to "direct affairs," nor yet with the conviction that Abraham Lincoln "should reap the honors due chiefly to his labors," but because any idea of political preferment was to him utterly hopeless. It is an incontrovertible truth that he had the confidence and support of no party, and was consequently wanting in that power which derives its strength from public opinion.

Perhaps no one occurrence better illustrates the executive and administrative course of Mr. Seward, than certain proceedings in relation to mails taken on captured vessels. Very little publicity was given to the subject at the time, though it was the cause of frequent and earnest discussion, and of a somewhat extensive and elaborate correspondence.

I received on the last day of October, 1862, a brief note from Mr. Seward, saying: "It is thought expedient that instructions be given to the blockading and naval officers, that in case of capture of merchant vessels suspected or proved to be vessels of the insurgents or contraband," the mails should "not be searched or opened, but be put as speedily as may be convenient on the way to their designated destinations." By whom it was "thought expedient" that such illegal "instructions" should be given, and an essential national right renounced in the midst of war when most needed, did not appear. The note, though characteristic, was of such a tenor that I gave it no attention whatever, except to say to Mr. Seward within a day or two, probably at our next meeting, that I had received it, that I disliked its tone, and knew not its object, or whether it was private or official, but it could not be expected I would carry it into effect. He made a passing reply that he had great difficulty in keeping the peace and satisfying foreign demands, particularly the English, who were very exacting. There the matter rested, and I supposed was ended; but six months later he came to my house, Saturday evening, the 11th of April, with a letter from Lord Lyons enclosing an extract from Mr. Archibald, the English Consul in New York, who had written his lordship that the mail-bag of the Peterhoff, a captured vessel, was in the prize-commissioner's office, "that the court had directed the mail parcels should be opened in order to see what letters were enclosed relating to the cargo on board the ship, and requested that I would open the package and select such letters as appeared to me to relate to the cargo on board or to the consignee mentioned in the manifest, and to take charge of the residue, with a view of forwarding them to their destination." With this request the consul refused to comply, and immediately informed Lord Lyons, who wrote Mr. Seward that "all these proceedings seem to me to be so *contrary to the spirit of your letter* to the Secretary of the Navy of the 31st of October, that I cannot help hoping you will send orders by telegraph to stop them."

I asked Mr. Seward if he had telegraphed or written as requested. He said he had not; it was not strictly within the province of the State Department; the court would not be likely to be governed by anything from him on a subject of naval concern; he therefore wished me to send word to the court to give up the mail. I assured him I was not prepared to send any such order; that I could not do it without a violation of law, and that the judge knew his duty too well to regard such an order from him or me; that the mails were legally in the custody of the court, and ought not to be given up without examination, for, in all probability, the best, and perhaps the only evidence that the Peterhoff was a good prize, was to be found in the mail bag. It would be wrong toward the government and unjust to the captors to part with this evidence.

He was greatly disturbed; said he was committed by his letter to me of the thirty-first of October, which had directed and virtually pledged the government that the mails should be given up without search. I replied that he was not authorized to give any such direction or pledge; that it was contrary not only to usage but to international and statute law; that I had paid no attention to his note, which was irregular and improper, as well as illegal, subversive of usage, and an unauthorized abandonment of a national right, which would be most injurious to the navy and the country; that as regarded any personal humiliation in recalling or disavowing it, no one but myself was aware he had ever written such a note, and it had entirely passed from my mind. He answered that he had given a copy of it, and it had been read and received as authority in Parliament. Our government would be holden to the promise he had made. But, said I, you could make no promise to override the law, or against law; the letter was not an executive order, an act of Congress, or a treaty stipulation. I regretted that it had been written, still more that it was published, for it was supercilious and improper on his part to undertake to instruct the Secretary of the Navy as he would a subordinate; that it was unfortunate such a note, unofficial and of no authority whatever, should have been made public. It was discourteous for him to address such a letter to me; disrespectful and wrong to have communicated such an unauthorized missive to the English Minister; that they were not aware he was not empowered to instruct me or any of his colleagues; that this subject had never been a matter of Cabinet consultation, and was in no sense an administration measure. He left me at a late hour, and after a pretty earnest conversation, to see Lord Lyons. The Minister was unyielding, and the question was carried to the President, who frankly stated that the subject was new to him; that he was not familiar with maritime law or the law of prize. I turned his attention to our statutes, which were clear and explicit. The law of 1789, our earliest statute, says: " All papers, charter-parties, bills of lading, passports, and other writings whatsoever found on board any ship or ships which shall be taken, shall be carefully preserved, and the originals sent to the courts of justice for maritime affairs," confirmed by the law of 1800, and subsequent enactments.

Eminent counsel were consulted, and authorities hunted up, but the whole array was against the unauthorized, illegal, and ill-considered note of the thirty-first of October. For days and weeks the subject was under consideration, and the more clear and unquestionable the case appeared, and the greater the embarrassment of Mr. Seward, the deeper were the President's sympathies for him and the stronger his wish to extricate the Secretary from a dilemma into which he had been apparently unwittingly seduced. The transaction was studiously withheld from Cabinet consultations. Mr. Seward had, it seemed, in a weak and unguarded moment, attempted to show to Mr. Stuart, of the British legation, his authority and power as Secretary of State; that he was virtually the premier and the controlling mind of the Government; that he could issue orders to his associates in the Cabinet as he would to subordinates, and regulate international questions by a mere dash of his pen, without regard to the President and Cabinet, the Senate or Congress. But when the question came to a practical issue, and he was required to show his authority to make regulations for the navy, to set aside the laws of the country, to disregard international law and usage, his ill-timed letter and assumption of power came home with terrible effect. Law and usage and the practice of nations could not be overturned by a flippant note from the head of a department. Only an Act of Congress or a treaty duly ratified could do what the Secretary of State, with all the experience and superior intelligence awarded him by Mr. Adams, attempted to do, in order to gratify a subordinate in the British legation, who had an object in view, and gained his point by seducing the Secretary, whose vanity was susceptible. When I asked if this renunciation of a right, which would impair the efficiency of the navy and operate injuriously to our national interest, was reciprocal, whether the British Government had consented, in case of war, to also abandon the right, M. Seward admitted they had come under no obligation to that effect, but he had no doubt they would. His principal justification, however, was the unfriendly feeling of Great Britain, which he declared was very hostile, and that it was his constant labor and duty to pacify and appease that government. This necessity, he said, had driven him to extraordinary concessions, and in promising the surrender of the mails without examination he had acted in the interest of peace. In other words, he had disregarded law, renounced an essential right at a critical period of the war without reciprocity, without an equivalent, without Cabinet consultation, and submitted and yielded to the illegal exactions of the English legation.

Senator Sumner, chairman of the Committee on Foreign Relations, in whose superior intelligence and information on questions of international law President Lincoln had great confidence, and whom he often consulted on conflicting and troublesome subjects with foreign powers, became greatly interested in this question. He assured the President that the Secretary of the Navy was right, and the State Department wrong. But Mr. Seward insisted that the British Government was sensitive, and if we opened and examined the mails they would avail themselves of the occasion to make war. This the President dreaded. I claimed that the best way to avert war was a fearless maintenance of our rights; that to abandon or renounce our rights from fear or threat would be humiliation and weakness. The point was one on which the President assumed the Secretary of State must be correctly informed, and, horrified with the idea of irritating Great Britain, which Mr. Seward insisted would be inevitable, and all his sympathies being with the Secretary, he thought it expedient to accede to Lord Lyons' demand, and surrender the Peterhoff mails.

Mr. Seward did not call and inform me after the interview on the evening of Saturday, the 11th of April, of the result of his visit to Lord Lyons, but I received on Monday the 13th, a note from him enclosing a letter from the Minister, written on the 9th, with extracts from a correspondence between Rear-Admiral Bailey and the British Vice-Consul at Key West in which Lord Lyons said : " It would seem from these that the mail found on board the captured steamer Peterhoff has been dealt with both at Key West, and at New York in a manner which is *not in accordance with the views of the government of the United States as stated in your letter* to the Secretary of the Navy of the 31st of October last." Mr. Seward's letter, enclosing this correspondence was written on Saturday the 11th, before his evening interview with me at my house and previous to his reception of the second letter from Lord Lyons, which he brought to me, with notice from Mr. Archibald stating the mail was in the hands of the prize-commissioners. This letter of the 11th reached me on Monday morning, and having in view our conversation on Saturday evening, I embraced the opportunity of sending him at once the following reply:

"NAVY DEPARTMENT.
April 13, 1863.
"SIR:—

"I have the honor to acknowledge the receipt of your communication of the 11th inst. enclosing a note of Lord Lyons' and correspondence relative to the mail of the Peterhoff.

"His lordship complains that the Peterhoff's mails were dealt with 'both at Key West and at New York in a manner which is not in accordance with the views of the government of the United States, as stated in your letter to the Secretary of the Navy, of the 31st October last.'

"Acting Rear-Admiral Bailey, an extract from whose letter is enclosed in the correspondence transmitted on the 14th ult., gave Her Majesty's Consul at Key West an authenticated copy of the law of the United States, and of the instructions based thereon, on the subject of papers which strictly belong to captured vessels and the mails. By special direction of the President, unusual courtesy and concession were made to neutrals in the instructions of the 18th August last to Naval officers, who themselves were restricted and prohibited from examining or breaking the seals of the mail-bags, parcels, etc., which they might find on board of captured vessels, under any pretext, but were authorized at their discretion to deliver them to the consul, commanding naval officer, or the legation of the foreign government to be opened, upon the understanding that whatever is contraband, or important as evidence concerning the character of a captured vessel, will be remitted to the prize-court.

"On the 31st of October last, I had the honor to receive from you a note suggesting the expediency of instructing naval officers that, in case of capture of merchant vessels suspected or found to be, vessels of insurgents or contraband, the public mails of every friendly or neutral power, duly certified or authenticated as such, shall not be searched or opened, but be put as speedily as may be convenient on the way to their designated destination. As I did not concur in the propriety or 'expediency' of issuing instructions so manifestly in conflict with all usage and practice, and the law itself, and so detrimental to the legal rights of captors, who would thereby be frequently deprived of the best, if not the only evidence that would insure condemnation of the captured vessel, no action was taken on the suggestions of the letter of the 31st October, as Lord Lyons seems erroneously to have supposed.

"In the only brief conversation that I ever remember to have had with you, I expressed my opinion that we had in the instructions of the 18th of August, gone to the utmost justifiable limit on this subject. The idea that our naval officers should be compelled to forward the mails found on board the vessels of the insurgents— that foreign officials would have the sanction of this government in confiding their mails to blockade-runners and vessels contraband, and that without judicial or other investigation, the officers of our service should hasten such mails, without examination to their destination, was so repugnant to my own convictions, that I came to the conclusion it was only a passing suggestion, and the subject was therefore dropped. Until the receipt of your note of Saturday, I was not aware that Lord Lyons was cognizant such a note had been written. Acting Rear-Admiral Bailey has acted strictly in accordance with the law and his instructions in the matter of the Peterhoff's mail. The dispatch of Lord Lyons is herewith returned.

"I am respectfully,
"Your obed't servant,
"GIDEON WELLES,
"Sec't'y of Navy."
"HON. WM. H. SEWARD,
"Sec't'y of State."

This letter exhibiting our different views and opinions, would I supposed, cause the subject to be brought before the President and Cabinet; but instead of this, Mr. Seward wrote me on the 15th, that he had submitted the subject to the President who approved his course, that the Peterhoff's mail was to be given up, and that it was an inauspicious time to 'raise new questions or pretensions under the belligerent right of search.' This hasty committal of the President was a sort of snap judgment so unlike him, and so inconsistent with his character and general course, that it was evident to my mind that confiding in the Secretary of State, he had given his sanction to the proceeding without a full knowledge of the facts, or of the irregular and illegal act which renounced our unquestioned right, and, if made a precedent, would work serious injury to the country. I was not willing therefore, that the question should be thus summarily disposed of nor to remain quiet under the admonition respecting 'new questions or pretensions.' The warning that Great Britain would take offence—an argument often used to affect the President on doubtful or disputed points by the State Department, I knew how to appreciate, and therefore wrote the following:

"NAVY DEPARTMENT.
April 18, 1863.
"SIR:—

"I have had the honor to receive your note of the 15th inst. in reference to the mails of the Peterhoff which are in possession of the prize-court in New York. I am not aware that this Department has raised any 'new questions or pretensions under the belligerent right of search,' in the case of the mails of the Peterhoff. Had there been ground for such an imputation, it could hardly, on an occasion to which so much importance has been given, have escaped the observation of Lord Lyons. He however, advances no such charge, directly or by implication, and founds the demand made by him exclusively on the concession which he, apparently through some knowledge of the details of your letter to me of the 31st October, had been erroneously led to believe was made by this government, in instructions given to the commanders of its vessels of war.

"The true question in the present case is, whether the administration of the law shall be suffered to take its ordinary course, or whether the court established to administer the law, and which has certainly been in existence long enough to know its powers and duties, shall be arrested in the discharge of its functions by an order of the Executive, issued on the demand of a foreign government, which exhibits no evidence, and in fact makes no charge that law or usage has been violated on our part.

"If the Peterhoff was captured and sent to the prize-court without any reasonable grounds for such a proceeding, then undoubtedly the opening of the mails, if it takes place, may have been an illegal act—but in my judgment, not otherwise. If it is to be assumed that the capture was wrongful, not only the mails, but the vessel and cargo should at once be surrendered.

"It may be an 'unfavorable time to raise new questions or pretensions,' but it is certainly no time to renounce any right or to unsettle any long and well-established principles and usage. Such a surrender would be a confession of weakness which, even if it existed, it would be inexpedient and injurious to make known to our enemies. If the case be one of doubt, it will be time enough to yield when the doubt is dispelled, and we are found to have been in the wrong. We may then yield and make amends.

"I do not consider it necessary to discuss the question of genuine or spurious and simulated mails; but will merely suggest that if what pretends to be a mail is to be considered, in all cases, *prima facie* sacred, and exempt from examination, it will hereafter be found exceedingly difficult, in practice, to distinguish the spurious from the genuine; nor indeed would there be any necessity for the fabrication of a spurious mail.

"In the meantime I cannot but hold that the prize-court is lawfully in possession of the mail-bag in question, and that the court itself is the proper authority to adjudge and determine what disposition shall be made of it. I propose to avoid all new questions by leaving the whole matter to this ancient method of adjustment, established by the consent of nations, and it was in order to avoid innovations, as well as to maintain our national rights and the legal rights of the captors, that

the suggestions contained in your note of the 31st of October were not adopted by this Department.
"I am, respectfully,
"Your obed't serv't,
"Gideon Welles,
"*Sec't'y of Navy.*"
"Hon. Wm. H. Seward,
"*Sec't'y of State.*"

Before sending this letter I read it to the President who was evidently surprised and somewhat disturbed by it. He said that the subject was one with which he was not familiar—that he had no time to investigate it and must depend on those of us who understood it, that his great object was to keep the peace which was much endangered, he thought it unnecessary to bring the matter before a full Cabinet—Seward he said was sensitive, he wished me to send Seward the letter, and if he did not bring it to his notice, which I doubted from what had already occurred, said he would call it up for further action.

At the Cabinet meeting on the 21st he requested Mr. Seward and myself to remain after the adjournment, and when we were alone, made known that his object was to get at the right of the question in relation to the seizure of foreign mails. A long and animated discussion took place in which Mr. Seward dwelt at length on the great changes which had taken place in regard to mails during the last fifty years, and that nations must move forward with the improvements of the age; spoke of the Trent affair and the concessions that were then made, of the necessity of keeping at this time on good terms with England and said, that the measures he had taken had been with the President's approval.

I thought it unnecessary to discuss the changes that had taken place in regard to the mails which constituted the principal part of his remarks, for whatever they were, law and usage and the practice of nations could not be set aside, except by legislation or treaty, denied that the Trent was a parallel case, and maintained that the legitimacy of the capture and the disposition of the mails belonged by law to the courts and not to the executive.

The President said he had no distinct recollection that the subject of captured mails had been brought to his notice, but Mr. Seward was doubtless right for it was his work. The Trent case he did not consider analagous, but he thought the executive had perhaps some rights in the matter though he was not certain what they were, nor what had been the practice. The discussion closed by his saying he wished to be thoroughly informed on the subject, and in order to be informed and to hold us each responsible for our positions he would address to us certain interrogatories which we could respectively answer. Mr. Seward remarked that there was no time, that Lord Lyons was pressing him, claiming that we had conceded the point. I replied that Great Britian had no claim whatever except under his note of the 31st of October which I regarded as unofficial and of no authority until our statutes were repealed.

On the next day I received from the President the interrogatories addressed mutually to the Secretary of State and myself which I insert with my answer.

"Executive Mansion, April 21, 1863.
"Hon. Secretaries of State and Navy.
"Gentlemen,
"It is now a practical question for this government whether a government mail of a neutral power, found on board a vessel captured by a belligerent power, on charge of breach of blockade, shall be forwarded to its designated destination, without opening ; or shall be placed in custody of the prize-court to be in the discretion of the court, opened and searched for evidence to be used on the trial of the prize case. I will thank each of you to furnish me :

"First, a list of all cases wherein such question has been passed upon, either by a diplomatic or a judicial decision,

"Secondly, all cases wherein mails under such circumstances have been without special discussion either forwarded unopened, or detained and opened in search of evidence. I wish these lists to embrace as well the reported cases in the books generally, as the cases pertaining to the present war in the United States,

"Thirdly, a statement and brief argument of what would be the dangers and evils of forwarding such mails unopened,

"Fourthly, a statement and brief argument of what would be the dangers and evils of detaining and opening such mails, and using the contents, if pertinent, as evidence,

"And lastly, any general remarks that may occur to you or either of you.
"Your Obed't Serv't,
"A. Lincoln."

"NAVY DEPARTMENT,
April 25, 1863.

"SIR :—

" I have the honor to acknowledge the receipt of your communication of the 21st inst. in which you direct me to furnish certain information, which is called for by you in consequence of the application made by the British Minister, Lord Lyons, for the delivery without examination by the prize-court, of the government mail found on board the Peterhoff ; a British vessel recently captured and brought into the port of New York.

" This application had previously been made known to this Department, and was urged upon it not as a request, but, as I understood, a demand founded on a communication by which a right is assumed to have been yielded by this government.

" It is, I believe, nowhere claimed by Lord Lyons or the parties in interest, that by any law or usage of this or any other country, or by any principle or practice among nations that this examination should not be made, but it is urged, or demanded that the mail shall be given up and the evidence essential to condemnation surrendered, by reason of a letter from the Secretary of State, under date of October 31st, 1862, addressed to the Secretary of the Navy, suggesting instructions to our naval officers. The proposed instructions would in my judgment have been such a renunciation of the rights of the nations and of the captors that the suggestions were never carried into effect.

" The pretension that mail-bags found on board vessels captured at sea, should be exempt from examination by a prize-court appears to the Department not only novel and startling, but, if admitted, pregnant with the most serious consequences. A recognition of it would seem to be nothing less than a surrender of all the rights of the captor government in such courts.

"The Department, after inquiry, can find no precedent for such a pretension—no case in which it has been either asserted diplomatically or affirmed judicially. The right of examining all papers, of whatsoever nature, found on board a captured vessel appears to have been always exercised.

"Our own earliest statute on the subject, the Act of March 2, 1789, for the Government of the Navy directs that:

"'*All papers*, charter-parties bills of lading, passports, and *other writings whatsoever*, found on board any ship or ships which shall be taken, shall be carefully preserved, and the *originals* sent to the courts of justice for maritime affairs.'

So too the Act of April 23, 1800:

"'The commanding officers of every ship or vessel in the navy, who shall capture or seize upon any vessel as a prize, shall carefully preserve all the papers and writings found on board, and transmit the whole of the originals unmutilated to the judge of the district to which such prize is ordered to proceed.'

"Our law on this subject is borrowed from the British law and practice. The instructions of the King to commanders of letters-of-marque, issued September 29, 1798, direct them to bring and deliver to the admiralty judge:

"'All such papers, passes, sea-briefs, charter-parties, bills of lading, cockets, *letters and other documents and writings* as shall be delivered up 'or *found on board* any ship.' (2 Rob. Appendix No. VIII.)

"It has never been pretended that these instructions, which except no letters or papers whatsoever, whether contained in mail-bags or not, are in violation of international law. And yet for what purpose are all the letters and writings found on board, without exception, to be delivered to the admiralty judge if not to be used as evidence in the case?

" The 'standing interrogatories' administered to all witnesses in every prize, British, or American, direct them to state under oath,—16th Interrogate—'What papers, bills of lading, *letters or other writings* were on board the ship at the time she took her departure from the last clearing port, before her being taken as a prize? Were any of them burnt, torn, thrown overboard, destroyed or cancelled, or attempted to be concealed, and when, and by whom, and who was then present?'

" What necessity could exist for destroying or attempting to conceal 'letters or other writings' if, by simply enclosing them in a mail-bag, they were exempted from examination? The very reason for destroying or attempting to conceal them is, that the mail-bag is *not* exempt from examination by the court. And the very reason for making it all important to seek and find the information concealed in letters is, that without such information, there would hardly in any case be sufficient proof to condemn a vessel. So far as it respects the ordinary ship's papers—clearance, manifests, etc,, every vessel would appear innocent.

" No rule can be better known,' says Sir Wm. Scott, 'than that neutral masters are not at liberty to destroy papers; or if they do, that they will not be permitted to explain away such a suppression by saying they were only private letters.' (The Two Brothers, 1 Rob. 134.)

" This rule, so well known, must have originated from the practice of destroying papers, and such practice necessarily implies the practice of searching for, seizing and sending in for judicial examination all papers, including 'private letters.'

"The British practice of seizing such private letters and using them in evidence in the prize-court will appear from the case of the Romea (6 Rob). The report of the case shows that the commander of a British gunbrig, in the exercise of the right of search, had stopped an American vessel,' 'had examined her papers and finding a letter which purported to disclose the real state of a transaction which had been fraudulently concealed, had sent the paper in question to the King's proctor, officially, but without detaining the ship in which it was found.' The letter was a private letter having no relation to the vessel in which it was found, or the cargo of that vessel, but, relating to another vessel.

"In the case of the Atlanta (6 Rob.), Sir Wm. Scott refers to the case of the Lisette 'which had carried a Dutch packet in the Danish *mail-bag*.' How could this have been known but by examining the Danish mail-bag?

"In the case of the Caroline (6 Rob.) dispatches from the Minister and Consul of France in the United States to the government of France were found on board an American vessel. As it had never been decided and was not in this case decided, that carrying such dispatches was ground for condemnation, it is presumed that these dispatches were not concealed on board the Caroline but found in the ship's letter-bag.

"The practice of our courts, so far as is known, has been in conformity with that of the British. Our statute peremptorily directs that all 'papers and writings found on board' a captured vessel shall be sent to the district judge. The Department is not aware of any exception taken to this law until very recently; though in the numerous captures which have been made during the present war, mail-bags containing important correspondence must have been frequently transmitted to the prize-court. If there had been any violation of international law or usage in this course it is not to be doubted that we should have been very promptly reminded of it, and in earnest terms. Yet it is not until near the close of the second year of the war, that anything in the nature of a remonstrance appears, and then the remonstrance is, not against a departure from international law or usage, but against the tenure of a surrender of an independent and established right made and communicated to the British Minister without alleged authority from the President, and as is believed by this Department, in direct contravention of the ancient policy of this and other governments, and of the rights and duties of captors as defined by statute.

"That there may be in the discretion of the prize-court some exception to an indiscriminate examination of all letters and writings found on board of a captured ship, may be admitted in cases when such exception does not interfere with the proper evidence; and no doubt such exceptions have been made in practice in favor of official dispatches. They have been regulated, however, not by strict international law, but rather as a matter of comity between nations.

"If a mail-bag on board a captured vessel is to be held sacred and free from judicial examination, what security will there be that it does not conceal and protect the proof which the captor requires to condemn his prize, and which would be sufficient to condemn it? No government could give such assurance without a previous examination of all the private letters admitted into the bag. Few private individuals would be content to have their letters examined by government officials, before being admitted into the mail, although they might be willing to run the risk of their being examined by belligerents during the war.

"And if individuals are willing to run this risk, why should their government insist on protecting them against it? Why indeed, should the most exacting government insist on anything more than that its own dispatches, certified as such, or claimed as such by responsible officers, should, when known to be such, be free from scrutiny. There would be little difficulty in framing an arrangement to this effect.

"No such arrangement is now in existence, except, as before stated, informally, perhaps by custom, and in conformity with the comity due to friendly or neutral governments in reference to their admitted official dispatches.

"The instructions which were issued by this Department on the 18th August last, to commanders of vessels of the Navy, authorizing them to use their discretion in delivering up government mails or dispatches found on board captured vessels, to be opened and examined in their presence, merely empowered them to exercise a comity towards neutral or friendly governments, the exercise of which might be safely entrusted to those who were on the spot, had the means of judging, and being interested in the capture, were not likely to show undue indulgence. The only doubt entertained by me as to those instructions was, whether they were in strict conformity with our statute and with the rights of the captors. But in deference to the State Department communicating with foreign powers, it seemed possible to presume that the Executive government here might have so much discretionary power in such cases.

"These instructions, however, I considered a stretch of power on the part of this Department, and even of the Executive, and when it was proposed shortly afterwards that they should be put in the form of a positive injunction to forward immediately to their destination all government mails found on captured vessels, a very little reflection sufficed to convince me that no such order ought to be issued.

"But unfortunately, it has been taken for granted that a mere suggestion made without alleged authority by the President, and by this Department at once objected to, was carried into immediate execution; and what is more unfortunate, at least one foreign government has been led apparently to adopt the very same erroneous conclusion.

"Such presumption is wholly unathorized and is incompatible with the nature and organization of our government. Under our constitution and laws the Chief Magistrate gives, or is supposed to give, directly to the head of each of the principal departments his orders in relation to the business of the departments respectively, and this most especially in all matters of *national* importance.

"And in all matters—especially important matters—affecting the *international* relations of the government, or its rights as a belligerent, even the Chief Magistrate might hesitate to adjust questions by an executive order, but would prefer to make them the subject of reciprocal treaty stipulations, duly considered and clearly expressed to be submitted to the scrutiny of the body whose concurrence is necessary.

"There is nothing to justify the presumption that this government would at a time like the present, surrender any of its belligerent rights by an executive order, in pursuance of a mere suggestion, not even reciprocal in its nature, and especially when such concession would effectually deprive it of all the advantages of the right of search.

"It is remarkable that in our traditional anxiety to

protect in treaty stipulations at every point all the rights of neutrals, we have never attempted to reserve mails, or mail-bags, or mail-matter from the scrutiny of a prize-court. On the contrary we have always recognized that by the law of prize, mail-matter may be contraband—for enemy's dispatches are mail matter and no prize-court in the United States, or in any other country, has ever doubted that they were contraband. In our treaty with New Granada we stipulate for the inviolability of correspondence on its land transit across the isthmus from ocean to ocean, but we abstain from attempting to make it inviolable on the sea. In our treaty with the Argentine Republic we stipulate, reciprocally the free access of mail-packets to the ports of the contracting parties, but there is no record in the treaty, excepting them or their mail-bags out of the belligerent right and law of search and judicial examination. On the contrary, Hautefeuille—perhaps the most eminent living publicist of France, and known as preëminently the champion of the rights of neutrals—in his very last publication, elicited by the affair of the Trent, does not hesitate expressly to affirm, that no mail steam-packet can, in its quality of a regular and recognized government mail-carrier, claim immunity from search, and much less of course from judicial examination. In the war with Mexico we, as a mere favor, permitted the ingress of British mail-steamers into Mexican blockaded ports. The mail-steamer Teviot abused the indulgence by carrying in the Mexican General Parades. We thereupon asserted diplomatically, our right both to condemn the Teviot and to withdraw the privilege from all the mail-packets. The British government made no denial of our position and settled the matter satisfactorily. [Mr. Bancroft to Lord Palmerston, Oct. 8, 1847.]

"On these grounds of judicial authority, of ancient practice, of statute law, and of public policy embodied in treaty stipulations, it is considered to be clear and unquestionable, that, in every case of capture of a ship upon probable cause, every manuscript, or printed paper found on board of her is liable in law to the inspection of a prize-court. Indeed a part of the complaint of the British government in the case of the Trent was, that the vessel was not brought in for adjudication in order to enable the court to determine whether or not she be a good prize. It cannot be otherwise—for being so captured, the ship is presumed to be in *delicto*—to be *pro hac vice*, adhering to the enemy—by some form of violation of the belligerent right of the captor government; and this predicament of the ship necessarily opens to the tribunal all the proofs of guilt which the ship contains.

"But all this, though conclusive, is not the most important point involved in this inquiry. That point is *not* the immunity of a government mail-bag from inspection by a prize-court, but it *is* the far higher and graver point of the immunity of the jurisdiction of the prize-court itself from executive interference. This transcendent question has been fully settled by the unanimous and unquestioned assent of all the departments of this government. By the constitution and by the law, our prize-courts, unlike those of England and other European powers are not a portion, or an appendage, or a dependent of the political administration, but are a part of the permanent organization of the judicial power, and invested with its independence in the determination and application of the law to all the cases of which they take cognizance.

"In a whole series of treaties, beginning with the Convention with France in 1800, and continuing down to our latest treaties with Spanish America, we solemnly stipulate that the prize-courts of the contracting parties shall have exclusive cognizance and adjudication of all questions of prize, and in case of condemnation, shall render, and on demand certify, to claimants the grounds of such condemnation.

"In our proclamation opening New Orleans and other ports to vessels from foreign ports, licensed by our consuls under authority of the President, we insert as a condition of the license that the vessel shall carry no information useful to the enemy, and the condition of her clearance by our own collector for her return voyage is, that he shall be satisfied and certify that in entering the port, she has complied with the requirements of her license. Must not the collector then have authority to inspect the mail she brings? And if our collector in execution of our municipal law has such authority, can we doubt that the prize-court has it under the broader belligerent right of search and the law of war? In our recent treaty with Great Britain respecting the slave trade, negotiated by the present Secretary of State, the reciprocal right of search, established by that treaty contains no exemption of mails, or mail-matter from such search. Suppose the Peterhoff had been brought in on suspicion under that treaty, is there a doubt that every paper on board of her could, in the discretion of the court, be looked into in order to settle the question of her guilt? We must remember that this question of the mail on board of a captured ship is a question of evidence against her. If the District Attorney may lawfully threaten the court, that he will abandon the case if the court looks into such evidence by reason of its being under an official seal, or lock, why may he not also in his discretion make the same threat to the court on the question of its inspecting any other official paper—the register, or clearance for example—which the ship contains? But by the whole law all this is settled otherwise. It is for the court under the law, and not for the Executive, to determine what papers found on board the prize-ship shall be inspected as evidence.

"No muniment by a foreign government can shield any writing whatever found on board a captured ship from such inspection, when deemed necessary by the court in the due administration of justice.

"In repeated cases, and without doubt or denial, the Supreme Court of the United States, with the full sanction of the Executive, has sat in judgment on the question, not of inspecting for evidence the government mail-bag, but as condemning as good prize a regularly documented vessel, or commissioned armed vessel, composing part of the navy of a foreign friendly power. Three of these cases—that of the Cassius in the 2d of Dallas, and that of the Exchange in the 7th of Cranch and that of La Jeune Eugenie, are reviewed by Mr. Attorney-General Wirt in an official opinion given by him in the year 1821. In these cases not only the foreign Minister claimed, *but the President was fully satisfied*, that the court could not condemn without infraction of the sovereign right of a friendly power by reason of the public character and commission of the ship. What happened? Did the President direct the court to release the ship, or not proceed to adjudication? Did the District Attorney threaten to abandon the case if the court should proceed? Quite the contrary. The President, *through the Attorney-General*, came into court, and made suggestion for the consideration of the court, as a part of the fact in the case, that the Executive was satisfied the ship was a public ship—such suggestion, no way mandatory in its character, but leaving open to the unswayed determination of the court all the evidence and the whole question of prize or no prize, was the uttermost limit to which the Executive deemed it right to proceed. The very careful language of Attorney-General Wirt on this point merits your special attention. It may be found in vol. I of 'Opinions of Attorneys-General,' page 505.

"In the late case of the Amisted, 15 Pet. Rep., page 587, the claim of Spain made in virtue of its sovereign right, even when supported by the admission of our Executive, was to the great satisfaction of the country overruled by the prize-court, and the Executive did not contest the validity of its decree. [See for citation, with approval of these cases, Wheaton's Elements, second edition by Lawrence, page 969, et seq.]

"These cases are as strong as any which can possibly be imagined, to show the absolute independence of our prize-courts in the adjudication of the most transcendent claims of foreign sovereignties, when presented in cases of prize; and the acknowledged immunity of these tribunals from any species of dictation or interference by the executive government.

"In the presence of such precedents, is it not clear that the prize-court has full right to examine the mail-bag found on board of a captured vessel, which doubtless contains conclusive evidence of her liability to condemnation?

"I observe that the terms of your letter refer only to vessels captured for alleged violation of the blockade. I suppose this restriction to be accidental, and that you intend the inquiry to extend to mails found on board of vessels captured for any cause as prize of war. The case of the Peterhoff, as I understand it, is not one of violated blockade, but a case of contraband.

"I observe also that your letter makes no reference to the question as to which department of the government is the proper organ to convey any suggestion from the President to the prize-court; nor does it refer to the question which of the heads of department is the statutory organ of the President to convey instructions to the District Attorneys of the United States. It is in my opinion important to the interest of the public service and to the good order of executive business, that there should be no conflict or misapprehension as to the character of the instructions to such officers, and I therefore beg leave to refer you to the recent Act of Congress of August 2, 1861, which in the pressure of your cares may have escaped your attention. It places the District Attorneys, in the conduct of all their official business, under the exclusive superintendence and direction of the Attorney-General, as the organ of the President.

"The court had it appears no hesitation as to its rights and duty to examine the mails of the Peterhoff, nor had the District Attorney. The court was proceeding to exercise its duty in conformity to law and usage when it was estopped by an order to the District Attorney—not emanating from, or conveyed through that department of the government to which he is by law attached—directing him to demand the surrender of the mail and with it of course the evidence therein contained.

"Now if the mails or captured vessels are to be forwarded to their designated destination, without inspection, and the evidence which they contain thereby denied to the captors, should not the chief law officer of the government be aware of the authority for so extraordinary a proceeding, whereby important national rights have been renounced and the rights of captors surrendered? It appears to me that if the suggestions of the

31st of October, which effect so great, and in my judgment so calamitous a revolution in the law of search, capture and adjudication, are to govern our national forces, that not only the officers of the navy, but the District Attorneys, the judges, and all authorities of our own and other countries should be promptly informed of this great change of policy, by an immediate and formal publication to that effect.

'In conclusion, I have no doubt that, even under the British rule as laid down in Earl Russell's recent communication to Mr. Spence, the Peterhoff, was rightfully captured and is liable to condemnation for carrying contraband, ostensibly to Matamoras, but with contingent destination to Brownsville. I still hope that sufficient evidence yet remains in the reach of the court to condemn this vessel and cargo, but I greatly fear that such evidence, even in this case may have been irreparably lost by the unfortunate surrender of the mail. However this may be in the present instance, I cannot doubt that if this case becomes a precedent, in future all documentary evidence to condemn any such ship will be concealed in her mail-bag, and no papers but innocent ones will be found outside of it. If so, condemnation of the guiltiest ship will become almost an impossibility while her capture may saddle her captors—who will only have done their duty—with heavy costs and damages, and probably the government with heavy claims for indemnification to the guilty party, whom its ill-ordered surrender of a clear right shall have enabled to conceal his guilt from the judicial eye.

"I most respectfully and earnestly invoke your serious and careful consideration of the evil consequences that must follow from this calamitous state of things. Already Mr. Spence, the Confederate Agent, has announced that the Peterhoff which had previously once run the blockade is but one of a line of four steamers, owned by him and destined to carry goods unquestionably contraband to Matamoras. The Peterhoff precedent, as it now stands, arms him with power to set at defiance all our efforts to stop such trade though its ultimate destination be undoubtedly to Brownsville ; for under this precedent, he will assuredly hereafter put the proof of the guilt of his vessels into the mail-bag and so beyond our reach. Thus, by our own act, done as I think in derogation of the unquestionable right of our prize-court, we shall furnish to our enemies an abundant supply of the munitions of war through the port of Matamoras. In this view I perceive with satisfaction that the prize-court has placed its surrender of the mail-bag exclusively, and only upon the request of the government, made known through the District Attorney. After careful consideration, I think that the court erred in yielding to this request, so expressed. I trust, however, that it is not yet too late for the government to retrieve its mistake, at least in part, by taking action and making such declarations as will prevent the case of the Peterhoff from becoming a precedent for the future surrender by the court of lawful and necessary evidence.

"If we go on as we have begun in the Peterhoff case, we shall find ourselves inconsiderately relinquishing an undoubted national right, not by consent of the people or with the approval of the government—not by treaty with reciprocal advantages, but by voluntary renunciation of an indispensable right in all naval captures in cases of contraband or breach of blockade.

"Besides national abnegation, a cruel wrong is done the gallant men of our navy, who will be liable to censure if they do not capture, and who are to be deprived by their own government of the evidence that would sustain them.

"I am Sir, with great respect,
"Your ob'd't serv't,
"GIDEON WELLES,
"Sec'ty of Navy."
"THE PRESIDENT."

Mr. Seward's answer to the the interrogatories I never saw, though I think the President promised me the perusal, or a copy, but the subject passed away, and I do not remember that it was ever again alluded to. Sometime after—about the close of the war, I met in the published deplomatic correspondence the following:

"DEPARTMENT OF STATE,
WASHINGTON, April 21, 1863."
"SIR :—
"The Peterhoff will be left to the care of the courts. Her mail will be forwarded to its destination unopened. I shall, however, improve the occasion to submit some views upon the general question of the immunities to public mails found on board of vessels visited under the belligerent right of search. The subject is one attended by many embarrassments, while it is of great importance. The President believes that it is not less desirable to Great Britain than it is to the United States and other maritime powers, to arrive at some regulation that will at once save the mails of neutrals from unnecessary interruption and exposure, and at the same time prevent them from being made use of as auxiliaries to unlawful designs of irresponsible persons seeking to embroil friendly states in the calamities of war.

"I am Sir, your ob'd't serv't,
"WILLIAM H. SEWARD."
"CHARLES FRANCIS ADAMS, Esq."

I need not comment on this letter, written months after the Secretary of State in his letter of the 31st of October had assumed without consultation or advisement to overturn and dispose of a long-settled question which involved the efficcient and proper administration of another department of the government and the government itself—an assumption in derogation of usage and a violation of law, on the ground that he deemed it expedient. In the workings and disposition of this subject the orator who delivered the "Memorial Address" has an exposition of that "solid power to direct affairs for the benefit of the nation through the name of another" which he asserts was exercised by Mr. Seward, a "superior in native intellectual power" to Mr. Lincoln. The latter anxious to extricate the Secretary of State and the country from its dilemma on becoming acquainted with the facts, the law and usage, thought it desirable that Great Britain and the other maritime powers should "arrive at some regulation" in regard to captured mails. He was not aware and Mr. Seward persisted in denying, that the question belonged to the courts, yet in the characteristic letter to Mr. Adams he admits "the subject is one attended by many embarrassments while it is of great importance." This important subject and its "many embarrassments" all of which by usage and international and statute law belonged to the courts, he, without consultation with the Cabinet, without the assent of the Senate, without the action of Congress, undertook to dispose of in a flippant letter to a subordinate of the English legation, by giving up without condition or equivalent our undisputed right. Worse than the original mistake, for it was doubtless a mistake of his authority, he refused to retract, and when he became informed, persisted in error to the detriment of the naval service and the injury of the country. What farther views, if any, he ever presented I am not informed. Nor, after our frequent passages on the subject, did he submit to me the letter addressed by order of the President, to Mr. Adams. The English government less willing to renounce a right than our Secretary of State, received with complacency our obsequious surrender in the case of the Peterhoff, but entered into no arrangement for renunciation on their part nor am I aware that the abandonment of our right was farther insisted upon after the subject was canvassed.

English enterprise, if not English diplomacy from the commencement to the close of our domestic difficulties was vigilant and unceasing in schemes to evade the blockade and establish intercourse with the rebels, of which the non-examination of the mails seemed a part. The western borders of Texas, where there was no military force to guard the frontiers, opened the way for illicit traffic which was hastily improved. The attention of the Secretary of State was repeatedly called to this subject with suggestion that we could not have a thorough blockade in the southwest under the existing state of things; but that an arrangement might be made with Mexico in relation to the navigation of the Rio Grande which was the boundary between the two countries, and that being a mutual highway, we could not close, nor could we but by consent of Mexico, interdict or regulate trade upon that river. An immense commerce sprang up with the neutral port of Matamoras which became for a period a great commercial mart, but it was notoriously illicit trade with the rebels through Brownsville. This fraudulent and evasive traffic was stimulated and encouraged by the assurance which the Secretary of State had given to England, of immunity to the mails. Information of this renunciation of our right of search was promptly communicated to the British public, by an announcement of the fact on the floor of Parliament. A line of British mail-packets to Matamoras, of which the Peterhoff, an old blockade-runner was one, was speedily established in the confident belief that a vessel with a mail and clearance to a neutral port, though carrying letters and freight fraudulently for Brownsville and the insurgent region, would escape capture, for the mails which could not be examined would cover the evidence of guilt. My suggestions that a treaty or arrangement might be made with the Mexican republic, by which we might blockade the Rio Grande were unheeded, lest we should give offence to Louis Napoleon who was sustaining the empire of Maximilian. The case of the Peterhoff and her mails demonstrated that a great diplomatic error had been committed. The Secretary of State had of his own motion, against law and without Cabinet consultation abandoned a national and indispensable belligerent right without an equivalent, without mutual arrangement or reciprocity. England would enter into no arrangement that required the surrender of the right which the Secretary of State had inconsiderately and without authority renounced. The act was our own. It was declared in Parliament that "Earl Russell considered that this was not an arrangement between her Majesty's government and the government of the United States, but simply an arrangement made by the government of the United States for the direction of their own cruisers."

Mr. E. Delafield Smith, District Attorney for the United States, who under direction of Mr. Seward withdrew the mail from the court and delivered it to the British consul also said in his argument before the United States court:

"The withdrawal from the registry of the court of the public mail of Great Britain and its delivery through us to the Consul of that country to be by him forwarded to its professed destination, will be cited by the respective counsel for the captors and the claimants. Each will insist that the mail might have produced witnesses in favor of his clients. As it was thus disposed of at my instance (under Mr. Seward), I shall argue nothing from its absence, and shall seek to infer nothing from the silence of the claimants when I applied for its release. *They* unquestionably in that silence acted in accordance with the wishes of *their* government, as I, in my application, *complied with the policy of my own.*"

A few days after the renunciation of our national right to placate England, Senator Sumner met Lord Lyons at the house of Tassara, the Spanish Minister, and expressed to him his regret that, taking advantage of the peculiar condition of our affairs, he should have made a demand on our government which could not be yielded without national dishonor; and remarked that the subject of examining all letters and papers on prizes was well settled by the law of nations, and that questions relating to mails on captured vessels were judicial rather than diplomatic. Lord Lyons disavowed ever having made a demand; said he was careful and guarded in all his transactions with Mr. Seward, and made it a point to reduce every question with him to writing. He authorized Mr. Sumner to examine his whole correspondence with the State Department; said he had of course been gratified with the voluntary renunciation by Mr. Seward of the right to search the mails; and when, contrary to the promise tendered by the Secretary of State, the mails were carried into court, he had called Mr. Seward's attention to his own letter of the 31st of October to the Secretary of the Navy, abandoning the right; but he had exacted nothing, made no demand, and merely asked him to do as he had promised.

When Mr. Sumner on the following day reported this interview with the British Minister, the President was filled with astonishment, and said, in his emphatic manner, "I shall have to cut this knot."

Of what advantage to the Executive or the country was the greater experience of the Secretary of State in this instance? He had been twelve years in the Senate, and by a dash of the pen, in a note of six lines, he, against usage—against both national and international law—without the action of Congress—without consulting President or Cabinet—without the consent of the people or the approval of the government—without a treaty with reciprocal advantages—without authority of any kind, assumed the power to relinquish and renounce an indispensable national right in naval captures. If the President, from friendship or sympathy, was influenced to shield or sustain the Secretary of State in his distressing embarrassment, it was under circumstances which will be rightly appreciated. It is one of many cases which exhibit the workings of the Administration— the " positive qualities" and real merits and course of action of the President and Secretary of State—the confiding nature of the former and the influence exercised by the latter; and from facts like these, a judgment may be formed how far the country and posterity are likely to " award honors to Mr. Lincoln that clearly belong to Mr. Seward." Let neither be robbed of the honors he earned, or of the just merits to which he is entitled.

The Peterhoff was an advance steamer of a proposed line of packets which were to convey mails and supplies, ostensibly to Matamoras, but with contingent destination for Texas. The whole scheme was deliberately planned to evade the blockade, and open for the rebels free communication abroad through British mails, via the Rio Grande; and the Secretary of State flattered and seduced, I need not say intimidated by the British legation, had without authority by law or by treaty, abandoned a principle and given the parties immunity by his ill-advised letter renouncing the national right to search the mails. After the mails of the Peterhoff were given up, that vessel or her appraised value was restored to her owners for the want of sufficient evidence to condemn her, a heavy loss to the captors and to the government; but the parties in the Matamoras line became involved in a legal controversy in the English courts after the war was over, when it was made evident that the vessel was actually good prize, and it is understood the evidence which would have insured her condemnation was in the mails that were surrendered.

DIFFERENCES existed in the Cabinet and the country in 1861 on some of the measures and the course of policy which the government should pursue toward the secessionists. The questions presented were in some respects novel and without precedent, as was the insurrection itself. Hostilities were precipitated within forty days of the inauguration, before the administration was fully established in place, or had time to develop its policy. The assault on the flag at Charleston compelled immediate action. The proclamation promptly issued for seventy-five thousand volunteers, also declared a blockade of the Southern ports. There was entire unanimity in the Cabinet on all points in the proclamation except that of a blockade, which was questioned as a doubtful and irregular proceeding; for the conflict, whether an insurrection or rebellion, was purely domestic—a civil war, and not a foreign war; and it was thought the internal dissensions in our own territory should be confined within our own borders. A majority of the Cabinet, therefore, preferred an embargo or suspension of intercourse with that part of the country, to a blockade, and maintained it to be the true policy of the government to close the ports and interdict commerce with the insurgents until the rebellion was suppressed. It was claimed that a blockade was not a domestic but an international question —legitimate and proper as between two distinct nations, but that we could not properly blockade our own ports, though we might shut them up, prohibit traffic from abroad by law, and make its violation a criminal offence ; that the very fact of a blockade of the whole rebel territory would raise the insurgents to the level of belligerents—a concession to the Confederate organization virtually admitting it to be a quasi government —giving that organization a position among nations that we would not and could not recognize or sanction, and which would inevitably lead to embarrassments. But the subject was in some of its aspects novel, and the Secretary of State, though sometimes rash, had not the bold and vigorous mind to assert and maintain a right principle, if fraught with doubt and difficulty, provided there was an easier path. The blockade, he thought, opened up a way. The questions of blockade were well settled and clearly defined, the authority and precedents explicit ; and he therefore preferred to adopt that course, shelter himself under those precedents, and apply international law to a strictly national and domestic controversy, rather than assert a measure and vindicate an important principle affecting national rights. Less was said, in the confusion and proceedings which came like an avalanche at that critical moment upon the Administration, than at a later period. Two members of the Cabinet, Messrs. Cameron and Caleb Smith said they had bestowed very slight examination upon the subject, and as it related to foreign intercourse they deferred to the Secretary of State, who had given it special attention, and also cited authorities justifying an exclusion of commerce from national ports in the equitable form of blockade. President Lincoln inclined to that view, and when Mr. Seward asserted that one great object of the blockade instead of a closure of the ports was to avoid complications which would be likely to involve us in a foreign war, the question was decided. The President said we could not afford to have two wars on our hands at once, and a blockade of our own ports and collection districts was ordered. The authority and the right of the national government to close ports within its jurisdiction was controverted by no one, though a blockade was. Mr. Seward himself, in his dispatch of the 8th of June 1861, to Mr. Adams, said: "We claim to have a right to close the ports which have been seized by insurrectionists for the purpose of suppressing the attempted revolution, and no one could justly complain if we had done so decisively and peremptorily." But the English Government, as soon as information crossed the Atlantic of differences in the American Cabinet, made haste to force us to adhere to the blockade, which would be an acknowledgment of belligerent rights to the rebels, by indirectly admonishing us of its views and intentions in a debate promptly got up in Parliament for the purpose on the 27th of June, immediately on the receipt of Mr. Seward's dispatch. Lord John Russell in that debate announced the interpolation of a new doctrine by the British Government into international law, by declaring to the feeble government of New Granada, "It is not competent for its government to close its ports that are *de facto* in possession of the insurgents."

The debate, ostensibly on the affairs of New Granada, was evidently and unmistakably intended as an admonition and menace to the United States, then engaged in suppressing insurrection. In a dispatch of the 28th of June from our Minister in London, just twenty days after Mr. Seward's dispatch of the 8th of June claiming our right to close the ports, Mr. Adams wrote the Secretary of State that in an interview with Lord John Russell, "His lordship then said something about difficulties in New Granada, and the intelligence that the insurgents had undertaken to close several of their ports. But the law officers here told him that this could not be done as against foreign nations, excepting by the regular form of blockade. He did not know what we thought about it, but he had observed that some such plan was likely to be adopted at the coming session of Congress in regard to the ports of those whom we considered as insurgents." His lordship also on the 27th of June announced in Parliament that "the opinion of Her Majesty's Government after taking legal advice is, that it is perfectly competent for the government of a country in a state of tranquillity to say which ports shall be open to trade and which shall be closed; but in the event of insurrection or civil war in that country, it is not competent for its government to close its ports that are *de facto* in the hands of the insurgents, as that would be an invasion of international law with regard to blockade."

Congress when it convened in special session in July, a few days after this English menace, totally unmindful of " the opinion of Her Majesty's Government after taking legal advice," but under the counsel and deliberate conclusion of our wisest and ablest legislators and statesmen, and in total disregard of the policy of our own Secretary of State as well as of Her Majesty's Government, declined to commit itself to the blockade, and in explicit and emphatic language authorized by the Act of the 13th of July, a closure of the ports. Mr. Seward was constrained, under these circumstances and under the direction of President Lincoln, on the 21st of July, to tell Mr. Adams that " Since your conversation with Lord John Russell, the Congress of the United States has by law asserted the right of this government to close the ports of this country which have been seized by the insurgents. The connecting by Lord John Russell of that measure when it was in prospect with what had taken place in regard to a law of New Granada, gives to the remarks which he made to you a significance that requires no especial illustration. The President fully agrees with Congress in the principle of the law which authorizes him to close the ports which have been seized by the insurgents, and he will put into execution and maintain it with all the means at his command, at the hazard of whatever consequences, whenever it shall appear that the safety of the nation requires it."

It is not expedient, perhaps, to follow up in its details a subject not particularly creditable to our diplomacy and to the maintenance of our national rights, further than to allude briefly to the historic facts. The brave words of the Secretary of State, uttered on the 21st of July, were not enforced. Mr. Adams, in a dispatch of the 16th of August, says he took occasion to intimate to Lord John Russell that "he must not infer from my not having entered into discussion of the merits of the question, that I gave any assent to the position taken by him about the right of a government to close its own ports, when held by forcible possession of persons resisting its authority. On the contrary, I desired to reserve for my government the treatment of it as an open question whenever it should take any practical shape. In the mean time I had every reason to believe that it was the design of the President to persevere in the blockade," etc. His lordship declared in Parliament, however, that he considered the law of Congress "as merely giving a discretionary power. But if carried into practice, he construed it as putting an end to the blockade." Under these threats our government tamely submitted. The law of Congress was not carried into effect, our diplomacy was meek and yielding, and under British menace the blockade of our own ports, by our own ships, was continued.

On the 2d of September the Secretary of State, with some trepidation, informed the Minister that "no change of policy in regard to the blockade has been adopted"—a timid intimation of acquiescence in an insult and injury, to appease British arrogance; her ministry believing and asserting that an effective blockade of our extensive coast was impossible, but that in no other way than by blockade could commerce be interdicted. Our government did not order the ports to be closed but under the hint given by the English dictum to New Granada, it abstained from exercising the national authority within that part of the territory of the United States that was in insurrection, and was passive and submissive. In all this time, while treating the Confederates as belligerents, and their organization as a quasi government, the Secretary of State, with strange inconsistency, denounced their cruisers as pirates.

Not until the 11th of April, 1865, after Richmond had fallen, and only three days before the assassination of President Lincoln, was a proclamation issued, in pursuance of the Act of Congress of the 13th of July, 1861, to close the ports of the Southern States. Until the war had virtually ceased, the law of Congress was not enforced. The British mandate to New Granada was submissively acquiesced in and obsequiously observed by the United States. Our ports were not closed, but blockaded, which eventuated, as was intended, in establishing throughout the war the English ports of Nassau, Bermuda, and Halifax as entrepots for illicit traffic with the rebels and resorts for rebel cruisers, to harass and destroy our commerce. It opened the English ports throughout the world to the Alabama, and rovers of her class, which swept our merchant ships from the ocean for the benefit of England.

On the subject of a blockade of our own ports by our own vessels, Mr. Seward had undoubtedly, for good or for evil, influence with the President, which outweighed a majority of the Cabinet and Congress. The subject was new to him when his decision was given, and the blockade being made effective by the navy, he did not care to re-open a disturbing question, though his views became modified, and ultimately the ports were closed, notwithstanding the English dictum to New Granada.

The management of our foreign affairs, and the maintenance of our rights against the pretensions and menaces of the arrogant ministry of England, thus commenced, was continued, until intelligent Englishmen themselves were surprised if not disgusted with our subserviency. After the shameful renunciation of our right to send into the courts, mails from captured vessels—a right recognized and established by the usage of nations, and made a duty by our own statutes—an eminent English publicist, Sir Vernon Harcourt amazed at our submissive and pusillanimous diplomacy, warned his government against proceeding too far in its demands, " for," said he; "*what we have most to fear is not that Americans will yield too little but that we shall accept too much.*" A humiliating commentary on our diplomacy, by an English writer of no mean ability.

The efforts of the secessionists to bring about a dissolution of the Union on the pretext that slavery in the states was in danger, in consequence of the success of the Republicans in 1860, and that new guarantees were required to protect the institution, had the effect of increasing the anti-slavery feeling in the free states. Until the attempts to secede from the Union and throw the country into dissevered sections, the fundamental law was strictly observed and adhered to throughout the whole North, and the right of each state to regulate its own affairs, its industrial pursuits, its domestic institu-

6*

tions, the condition of its people in the matter of servitude, of debtor and creditor, including imprisonment for debt, and punishment for criminal offences was respected. The serious agitation of the slavery question had its origin in fact with the nullifiers. After their defeat, as a party on the tariff issue and the futile claim of intolerable burdens by reason of high duties on imposts, which they had striven to make a political party test, the South Carolina politicians changed their tactics and professed to be greatly alarmed by the petitions of the Quakers and a few fanatics as extreme as the nullifiers themselves, and vastly inferior in numbers and talents, who—regardless of constitutional obligations and limitations, asked for the abolition of slavery by the general government.

So pronounced and universal was the sentiment of the North against this feeble sect, that politicians and public men denounced their doctrines and were careful to be in no way committed to, or connected with them. Abolition was as unpopular with both the great parties of the North as the South, but it pleased the Nullifiers to make indiscriminate war upon the free states and to classify the whole North as abolitionists inimical to the South and southern institutions. Disclaimers and disavowals were of no avail with the men who had a party purpose to accomplish by these deliberate misrepresentations. On the abstract question of slavery there was but one sentiment throughout the free states ; but this sentiment, for it was a sentiment—could not overcome the deep and sacred regard for constitutional obligations. On no political subject was there more unity, than that the rights of the states should be respected and observed on the question of slavery. But the Nullifiers started to be aggressive, and with a determination to be the ascendant party in the government or to subvert it. The means resorted to for uniting the South irrespective of parties on this local question were, by creating alarm in the slave states—stating the free states were aggressive—warning the slave owners that their property was in jeopardy—demanding new guarantees for its security—promoting sectional animosity and some of them requiring a dual executive.

Mr. Seward who, according to Mr. Adams, had in 1824 made "a deliberate claim of a right in the federal government to emancipate slaves by legislation," abandoned in the winter of 1861, this original position and proposed an amendment to the constitution guaranteeing the perpetuation of slavery so far as the general government was concerned by prohibiting Congress through all time and under all circumstances from exercising " any power to abolish or interfere in any state with the domestic institutions thereof, including that of persons held to service or labor by the laws of said state." Politicians of the Jefferson school, less practical, in the judgment of Mr. Adams, than Mr. Seward (for Jefferson never admitted "a right in the federal government to emancipate slaves,"), were averse to this extraordinary proposition which was presented as a peace-offering and a compromise by one who, according to the "Memorial Address" ought to have been made President instead of Mr. Lincoln.

When at length, after more than twenty years of declamation, agitation, persistent aggression and deliberate misrepresentation, the country became involved in civil war on the subject of slavery, it is not surprising that many who had until this time adhered to and maintained the constitutional safeguards, deprecated the cause of dissension and disunion and wished it removed. The rebellion rapidly increased the anti-slavery sentiment everywhere, and politicians shaped their course accordingly. On the wave of this anti-slavery excitement the Secretary of State and the British Minister in the spring of 1862 negotiated a treaty for the suppression of the African slave-trade, a revival of which had been threatened by the secessionists in the cotton-growing states. If other and ulterior purposes were designed, it was an adroit movement on the part of the English diplomat who availed himself of the popular feeling which in free governments influences public men. The Secretary of State very naturally fell in with a movement which was in harmony with public sentiment and the current of affairs. The treaty was quietly negotiated. I knew nothing of it until after its ratification, for it was not submitted for Cabinet consultation in any stage of its progress. When promulgated in the second year of the war, it did not create the sensation which might have been expected. Other and more exciting matters absorbed the public mind. There began to be a conviction that not only the slave-traffic but slavery itself was doomed. I do not remember to have seen or read the treaty until after it had been ratified and duly exchanged by both governments. A certified copy was sent me by the Secretary of State about the first of September, and also a copy of a singular arrangement, contract, or treaty negotiated or entered into by the Secretary of the Interior under advisement of the Secretary of State and the Charge d'affaire's of Denmark relative to the colonization in the West Indies of negroes captured under the treaty.

On the 17th of September I received the following letter from the Secretary of State with a list of some twenty or thirty naval vessels in Her Majesty's service, and a copy of the instructions of the British government to the respective commanders.

"DEPARTMENT OF STATE,
17 Sept. 1862."
"SIR:—

"I have the honor to invite your attention to the enclosed copy of a communication of the 13th inst. from the British Charge d'affaires here, embracing the instructions which it is intended to furnish to the commanders of Her Brittannic Majesty's cruisers who may be employed in carrying out the provisions of the recent slave-trade treaty between the United States and Great Britain as well as lists of Her Majesty's several ships employed on the African, North American and West India stations, whose commanders will be authorized to act under the treaty and asking for a similar list of United States cruisers.

"I am sir, your ob'd't serv't,
"WM. H. SEWARD."
"HON. GIDEON WELLES,
" *Sec't'y of the Navy.*"

This communication and the accompanying papers led to a critical examination of the treaty, which contained some extraordinary provisions that, if carried into effect, were likely to impair the efficiency of our own navy during the war. Whilst examining and considering the treaty, then wholly new to me, and concerning which I had not been consulted, although the navy was to be employed in carrying out its provisions; and in its operation our cruisers would be seriously affected by the instrument, I received a second or duplicate of the foregoing letter, hastening early compliance, and asking for a list of United States vessels with my instructions to officers commanding such as were authorized by the treaty to capture slaves. I replied on the 29th, informing Mr. Seward the treaty was wholly incompatible with the existing condition of affairs—that it would be impossible during the war to detail any vessel with specific instructions to act under the treaty, for it would, for belligerent purposes, destroy the efficiency of any vessel so instructed—that it would be virtually locking up a portion of the navy tying the hands of the government at a time when every vessel was wanted for blockade and independent cruising, and it appeared to me the full force and scope of the treaty could not have been well considered when negotiated. My letter was probably more pungent than was necessary or expedient. It aroused Mr. Seward's attention to certain conditions and stipulations, the operation of which had not attracted his attention while framing and assenting to the instrument. He evidently felt that he had been precipitate, and that there were unfortunate or unguarded stipulations in his arrangement with which we could not comply. He therefore wrote me an unofficial note on the 30th of September, enclosing the form of letter which he wished me to substitute for mine of the preceding day. His reason for this, as stated by himself was that he might wish to give Lord Lyons a copy of my objections which he saw were insuperable. But this proposed substitute prepared by him was gentle and too pointless in its expressions, and on the whole, of such a tenor that I was not inclined to adopt and make it my own, though desirous to oblige him in the emergency. I however modified my communication of the 29th and sent to him the following:

"NAVY DEPARTMENT,
"Oct 9, 1862.
"SIR:—

"I have the honor to acknowledge the receipt of your communications of the 17th and 26th ulto., enclosing a copy of a letter from the British Charge d'affaires, communicating the instructions which it is intended to furnish the commanders of Her Brittanic Majesty's cruisers who may be employed in carrying out the provisions of the recent slave-trade treaty between the United States and Great Britain, as well as lists of Her Majesty's several ships employed in the African, North American and West India stations, whose commanders will be authorized to act under the treaty, and asking for a similar list of United States cruisers.

"I have the honor to inform you that all our cruisers are at present exercising the belligerent right of search, and it would be highly detrimental to the service and unjust to the country to detach any of them at the present moment from the duties on which they are engaged and restrict their operations by instructions under the treaty for the present, or during the existence of hostilities, under the unquestioned belligerent right of search, each and all of our national vessels will exercise the rights which appertain to them as belligerents —will visit and search suspected vessels not only within the latitude prescribed by the treaty, but elsewhere; and in the exercise of this belligerent right, they will not hesitate to seize slavers or other piratical craft that are abusing our flag.

" To give our cruisers, now performing such general duties, instructions under the treaty, would be to limit their operations to a specific object, while the exigencies of the country require them to perform other necessary, legal and legitimate duties. So far as it is practicable on our part to use the belligerent right of search incidentally, in aid of the purposes of the treaty, we shall so use it.

" The important privilege of visit and search, and in some cases of detention and capture, is conceded by each of the two governments in this treaty, and offence cannot be taken at our waiving for a season the exercise of the privilege conceded. This waiver will not prevent British cruisers from searching and seizing suspected vessels claiming to be American, while those claiming to be English will also be searched by them. Besides this, our cruisers searching all vessels under the belligerent right, will of course capture all slavers which use or abuse the American Flag or adopt that of the rebels.

" I do not propose during the existence of hostilities to impair the efficiency or usefulness of our cruisers as war vessels by giving their commanders instructions under the treaty, for the reason that any naval officer acting under such instructions would be restrained from the general belligerent right of search—the instrument itself compels him to declare, on boarding a vessel, that '*the only object of the search,* is to ascertain whether the vessel is employed in the African slave-trade, or is fitted up for that trade'—whereas, instead of confining our officers to that only object in this time of war, we have not a cruiser afloat whose commander is not under imperative orders to search all merchant vessels for contraband of war. We can not consent to abandon the belligerent right of search and seizure, in the West Indies, where neutral obligations are disregarded and neutral flags are prostituted to aid the insurgents—consequently, I must for the present omit to issue any instructions under the treaty which permits no commander having instructions under the treaty to search a vessel in certain localities *for any other purpose* than that of detecting slaves.

"Whenever the condition of affairs will permit us to set apart cruisers for the special service required, it will give me pleasure to furnish a list of them as requested and to perform the duties which devolve upon the department for a strict execution of the treaty.

"I am, respectfully,
"Your Obed't Serv't,
"Gideon Welles,
"*Sec't'y of the Navy.*"

"Hon. W. H. Seward,
"*Secretary of State.*"

I on the same day addressed the subjoined communication, adverting to the unfortunate complications and difficulties in which we were likely to become involved by this confused mixture of executive, legislative and diplomatic proceedings, under the treaty, under the law of Congress which he had procured to be enacted, and under the Danish treaty which had never been ratified.

"NAVY DEPARTMENT,
Oct. 9. 1862.

"SIR :—

"Since the receipt of your unofficial note of the 30th ultimo, with the proposed form of a draft as a substitute for my letter of the 29th ultimo, I have given the subject much thought and examination. That a copy of my letter would have to be communicated to the British Government had not occurred to me. That fact, and some defects of full explanation in my letter of the 29th ultimo to you, render it proper that I should revise and modify my communication.

"I have therefore prepared the enclosed with some care, as better adapted, I think, to the case than the form you were so kind as to send me. This whole subject has become strangely complicated; there is, in the first place, the conceded privilege of reciprocal search by the treaty, and there is the unquestioned belligerent right of search which cannot be surrendered. Yet the two are in conflict. Then we come in contact with that strange anomaly, a treaty with Demmark, which has never been ratified by the Senate—concluded and signed by the Danish Charge d'affaires on behalf of the government of Demmark, and by the Secretary of the Interior on behalf of the government of the United States—not negotiated in conformity with the requirements of the Constitution, nor through the department that is charged with the special duty of making treaties, but by an entirely different department and under an Act of Congress which assumes to authorize the treaty or agreement regardless of the Constitution.

" The treaty with Great Britain provides that instructions shall be given to our cruisers. The form of letter which you send me promises that orders will be given for captured slavers to be sent into port for adjudication according to the terms of the treaty, and this without instructions.

" The mixed commission under the treaty cannot adjudicate the questions, if instructions are not given, and are precluded from action.

" In addition to this, by the Danish treaty or agreement, it is stipulated to the effect that all negroes, mulattoes, or persons of color on board of vessels seized in the prosecution of the slave-trade shall be sent to *West End*, in the Island of St. Croix, and our commanders, exercising the belligerent right of search, are to be instructed accordingly.

" It is true that this strange, unconfirmed and singular instrument makes no provision for adjudication and condemnation of any captured slaver. Ordering the negroes to be sent to St. Croix, therefore, may not be inconsistent with a condemnation under the treaty, but how can the slaves and slaver be brought before the mixed commission established by the treaty, when they are not captured by officers instructed under that instrument—such instructions being made a condition-precedent under that instrument, of all proceedings by the mixed commission?

" I find myself, I confess, embarrassed in several respects by the stipulations and complications involved in this subject of captured slavers, and see no other course to pursue, than to wholly abstain from any action whatever under the treaty, so long as the war continues.

" The privilege of reciprocal search for slavers being

conceded by the treaty, I do not see that the English government can complain if we do not avail ourselves of it, but permit them to enjoy it.

"Incidentally our own cruisers will, with greater energy and effect, aid in enforcing the object of the treaty under the more comprehensive belligerent right of search.

"It appears to me that this whole subject of slaves and slavers has become so involved and complicated by treaties and agreements and statutory enactments—the reciprocal right of search, and belligerent right of search—the process of adjudication under the mixed commission, under the stipulations to adjudicate by the British treaty, and the arrangements to send the negroes to St. Croix under the Danish agreements, that some measures should be adopted to disembarrass the question.

"I am, respectfully,
"Your Obed't Serv't,
"GIDEON WELLES,
"*Sec't'y. of the Navy.*"
"HON. WM. H. SEWARD,
"*Sec't'y. of State.*"

Whether a copy of my letter was ever sent to Lord Lyons is problematical, but he was made aware that the Secretary of the Navy was disinclined and believed it impracticable to carry out the stipulations of the treaty during the existence of hostilities. It was unquestionably an unpleasant topic to one of the temperament and mind of the Secretary of State to dwell upon, nor was it pleasant for him to admit that in a treaty on which he prided himself, he had committed an error or been overreached. I supposed at the time that the exceptional provision was an inadvertence on the part of both the negotiators, and have no doubt it was as regards the Secretary of State, but subsequent developments in regard to the treatment of mails captured and the simultaneous establishment of a line of British mail-packets to the Rio Grande, which was within the prescribed latitudes, where naval vessels under treaty instructions could *only* search for slaves, rendered it doubtful whether the English legation had not shrewdly availed itself of the zeal of the Secretary of State against slave traffic to adopt a measure which would promote English commercial enterprise by securing immunity to their vessels and thus opening a way for intercourse with the blockaded rebels.

Mr. Seward did not submit to me his letter to the English legation stating the obstacles which intervened to prevent the consummation of the treaty or action under it in the existing state of things, nor do I think the President was fully apprised of it. I only know that the treaty was necessarily suspended. The tenor of his communication to Lord Lyons, I learned some eighteen months later from the following letter, written several weeks after my communication of the 9th of October, stating the objections to issue instructions which would circumscribe and impair the rights and efficiency of our cruisers.

"WASHINGTON, November 27, 1862.
"SIR:—
"Mr. Stuart did not fail to communicate to her Majesty's government the note which you did him the

honor to address to him on the 14th of last month, and in which you stated certain reasons which induced the government of the United States to decline, for the moment to issue to commanders of United States vessels the instructions contemplated by the treaty of the 7th of April last for their guidance in carrying out the stipulations of that treaty for the suppression of the slave trade. The principal reason for omitting to issue the instructions appears to be an apprehension that they would restrict the more extended right of search, which the commanders of United States vessels now exercise as belligerents.

"And it seems to be believed that the object of the treaty may be in great measure attained by the exercise of this belligerent right of search in lieu of the special right of search provided for by the treaty. I am however instructed by Her Majesty's principal Secretary of State for Foreign Affairs to take an opportunity of representing to you, that although United States cruisers may search by virtue of their belligerent rights, yet they cannot by virtue of these rights, detain or send in for adjudication any neutral vessel not breaking blockade; in short, that they cannot give effect to the stipulations of the treaty unless they have such warrants and instructions as are prescribed by it.

"I have the honor to be, with the highest respect, sir, your most obedient humble servant,

"LYONS."
"HON. WILLIAM H. SEWARD,
 "*Secretary of State.*"

In this letter Her Majesty's principal Secretary of State did not controvert or modify the point presented, but denied that any neutral vessel, not breaking the blockade, could be detained or sent in for adjudication by the naval commander under the belligerent right— in other words, no slaver captured by our war-vessels without specific instructions, could be adjudicated by the courts established by the treaty, and if they had specific instructions, they could not capture blockade-runners or anything else. This ultimatum failed to influence our government, and from the necessity of the case, action under the treaty remained suspended.

Mr. Seward was, properly perhaps, opposed to any direct official communication between the representatives of foreign governments and the head of any department except through the Secretary of State. In this condition of affairs and while matters were in abeyance, Lord Lyons, a cool, adroit and sagacious diplomatist, but able and far-seeing, and I think, friendly to our government when it did not clash with British interests, felt it important that he should rightly understand the case and the difficulties to be overcome. As he could not, under the rule or practice, communicate with the Secretary of the Navy directly, he, on the 14th of December invited the Assistant Secretary of the Navy, Mr. Fox, to dine with him. Mr. Fox informed me of the invitation and that he had an intimation that Lord Lyons was anxious to know the difficulties in the way of carrying the treaty into effect. I authorized him to say frankly to Lord Lyons or any one else, that in declining to give special instructions which would tie up the hands of our naval commanders, my only object was not to impair their efficiency or circumscribe their undoubted belligerent right by specific instructions, that were inconsistent with the broader general belligerent right. Mr. Fox so informed the Minister, and in due time the treaty requirements were so far relaxed as to authorize a special warrant to our naval officers, to the effect that the rights and privileges under the treaty would not in any way derogate from or conflict with belligerent rights—that the power conferred by the treaty was added to belligerent rights, not substituted for them, and that the mixed courts of justice established by the treaty would exercise their functions in cases of captures under the belligerent right as well as the special right, which might be sent to them for adjudication. But, in point of fact, I believe not a single capture was made, the African slave-trade had ceased, and the cumbrous and expensive machinery of mixed courts at the Cape of Good Hope, Sierra Leone and New York were never put in operation. The officers of these tribunals never had anything to do but draw their salaries. After the war was over, the treaty, the Danish arrangement and all the accompaniments went out of existence. No great eclat attached to the negotiators of this slave-trade treaty in the United States, nor did Great Britain derive any commercial benefit from the attempt to limit the right of search below the latitude of 32°; but failing in this, of which the English legation was notified on the 14th of October, they succeeded on the 31st of that month in securing from the Secretary of State, without law, assurance of immunity to the mails. Lines of packets to Matamoras were immediately established, which opened intercourse to the rebel states through Texas and the blockade was thereby evaded.

That Mr. Seward himself came into the State Department with no acquaintance with the forms of business other than that obtained incidentally through his services in the Senate, is undoubtedly correct and is well exemplified in the whole arrangement attending this slave-trade treaty and its incidents, a treaty wherein the negotiator, represented as "a superior in native intellectual power" to the President and who exercised the more solid power to direct affairs "through the President's name," a treaty negotiated in the midst of war but which by its provisions would cripple the war power of the government, a treaty negotiated by the Secretary of State without consulting his colleagues in the administration, a treaty fortified or attempted to be fortified by an anomalous quasi-treaty entered into by another and a domestic department with the representative of a foreign government, which quasi-treaty or arrangement was never ratified by the Senate, as the constitution requires, but which anomaly and the law under which it was justified were the offspring of the negotiator of the slave-trade treaty and a part of that arrangement. This strange complication, the treaty, the quasi-treaty and the law, with the legal tribunals and the extensive and attending paraphernalia resulted in nothing but a large expenditure from the national treasury.

The subject of enlisting private enterprise in aid of the government upon the ocean as well as the land, early engaged attention. Vague and wonderfully exaggerated rumors that our commerce and shipping interests were endangered from swarms of privateers that were, or soon would be abroad, alarmed the mercantile communities, and stirred up the fishermen and mariners on our coast who were anxious that there should be counteracting movements against these threatened depredators. Schemes for a volunteer navy, propositions for a militia of the seas, tenders of yacht-squadrons and plans for naval brigades were pressed upon the government by men of position and character as well as by adventurous spirits. It was remembered that in the war of 1812 important service was rendered by the privateers. Without considering the difference between a foreign war with the wealthiest commercial nation and a civil conflict with insurgents who had neither commerce to be injured, nor booty to reward private enterprise, it was urged that the government might be benefitted now as then by reprisals.

The Secretary of State falling in with the current popular feeling favored these crude schemes; while the Secretary of the Navy who had more especially in charge, the police of the seas, questioned whether letters-of-marque could be made effective in this conflict with the rebels, and was apprehensive they might jeopard peaceful relations with other powers. At the commencement of difficulties the rebel government authorized the licensing of privateers which produced a great sensation and aggravated the existing hostile feeling. In the universal desire to strike the most effective blows against the rebels, the demand for using every available means became almost irresistible. Indications of a willingness by foreign governments, particularly by Great Britain, to give encouragement to the rebels by their treatment of questions of international maritime law had probably an influence on the Secretary of State and more deeply enlisted his sympathies with those who were zealous for carrying on upon the high seas, private as well as public war against the insurgents. No encouragement was given by the administration, for privateers, but the pressure from without, naturally led to occasional discussions in the Cabinet, which developed the different views entertained by the heads of the two departments most interested. But no decisive steps were taken, and this was in itself the naval policy. At the extra session of Congress in July, the subject was entertained by the members and among the acts passed conferring authority on the Executive, was one empowering the President to " authorize the commanders of armed vessels sailing under the authority of any letters-of-marque and reprisal granted by Congress—to subdue, seize, take, and if on the high seas to send into port."

But Congress omitted to authorize the issuing of letters-of-marque and prescribe conditions for the government of privateers; the enactment however served to relieve the administration in a measure from many of the schemes that had been urged. Shortly after Congress adjourned several highly respectable merchants of Boston engaged in the China trade, apprehensive that "rebel cruisers might get into those seas" addressed a communication to the Secretary of the Navy suggesting the " expediency of letters-of-marque or other commission," under the provision of the recent enactment. Application was also made to the Secretary of State by some of the same parties for letters-of-marque to the steamer Pembroke which was about sailing from Boston to China. Mr. Seward in view of the differences between the State and Navy Departments instead of answering this letter direct, referred it with an inquiry to me. My reply to him which the President approved, and which I here insert, corresponded with my answer to the merchants, and Mr. Seward disposed of the application to himself, by sending out and publishing my letter to him. This relieved him of responsibility.

"NAVY DEPARTMENT, Oct. 1. 1861.
" SIR :—

"In relation to the communication of R. B. Forbes, Esq., a copy of which was sent by you to this Department on the 16th ultimo, inquiring whether letters-of-marque cannot be furnished for the propeller Pembroke, which is about to be despatched to China, I have the honor to state that it appears to me there are objections to, and no authority for, granting letters-of-marque in the present contest. I am not aware that Congress, which has exclusive power of granting letters-of-marque and reprisal, has authorized such letters to be issued against the insurgents; and were there such authorization, I am not prepared to advise its exercise, because it would, in my view, be a recognition of the assumption of the insurgents, that they are a distinct and independent nationality.

"Under the Act of August 5, 1861, 'Supplementary to an Act entitled An Act to protect the commerce of the United States and to punish the crime of piracy,' the President is authorized to instruct the commanders of 'armed vessels sailing under the authority of any letters-of-marque and reprisal granted by the Congress of the United States, or the commanders of any other suitable vessels, to subdue, seize, take, and, if on the high seas to send into any port of the United States any vessel or boat built, purchased, fitted out, or held,' etc. This allusion to letters-of-marque does not authorize such letters to be issued, nor do I find any other act containing such authorization. But the same act, in the second section, as above quoted, gives the President power to authorize the 'commanders of any suitable vessels to subdue, seize,' etc. Under this clause, letters permissive, under proper restrictions and guards against abuse, might be granted to the propeller Pembroke, so as to meet the views expressed by Mr. Forbes. This would seem to be lawful, and perhaps not liable to the objection of granting letters-of-marque against our own citizens, and that too, without law or authority from the only constituted power that can grant it.

"I have the honor to transmit herewith a copy of a letter from Messrs. J. M. Forbes & Co. and others, addressed to this Department, on the same subject.

"I am very respectfully,
"Your obedient servant,
"GIDEON WELLES."
"WM. H. SEWARD.
"*Secretary of State.*"

The letter had the effect apparently of satisfying for a time, at least, those who had taken the deepest interest in the subject. But the ravages of the Sumter, which vessel was hailed with friendly welcome and supplied in British ports, with the subsequent depredations of the Alabama and Florida—English built, and manned chiefly by Englishmen, aroused the indignation of the whole country. This indignation was increased and aggravated by the conduct of the British government in excluding all United States cruisers from the English ports in China, though the seas of that empire were infested by pirates, and the whole commercial world was interested in their suppression. While our national ships in English ports received only grudging hospitality it was notorious that the semi-piratical vessels with no recognized nationality, though substantially English vessels sailing under the rebel flag were capturing, plundering and wantonly destroying our commerce, and that the injury to us was to the benefit of England. Under these wrongs and outrages our whole commercial marine became greatly excited, and could the country have been united, a war with England, more calamitous than any she had ever known, would have made havoc with her commerce. But our condition was such that forbearance became a duty, and the government while engaged in prosecuting a war with the rebels was also subjected to a severe trial, in restraining the popular demand for reprisals which would likely have begotten a war with Great Britain;—for though the crown was not unfriendly to the Union it was known that English capital was largely engaged in illicit traffic with the insurgents and in running and evading the blockade. At the same time the unnatural and unfriendly conduct of her ministry, who put forth no arm to prevent, but craftily connived at schemes against the Union was felt, and will be remembered against the Administration of Palmerston and Russell. It is some gratification to remember now when those dark days are over, that in addition to the award of fifteen millions for the criminal wrong we suffered from England, our navy, without assistance from privateers, captured more than thirty millions of property engaged in illicit traffic and running the blockade, no inconsiderable portion of which was English capital. While the public mind was inflamed by the wrongs inflicted, complaints were made of the want of efficiency on the part of the navy and Navy Department. Privateers, letters-of-marque were called for, regardless of the necessities of the case and of the consequences of committing to greedy and reckless adventurers the highest and most delicate responsibilities of government, an abuse of which would endanger our peace with other nations. To meet and dispose of these demands required decision and effort. The Secretary of State instead of repressing, quietly favored the privateer policy which had its advocates in certain persons and circles in New York. Fortunately the President, cautious but firm, maintained a prudent and wise reserve, and committed himself to no project that was likely to endanger the national welfare. There were also judicious and discreet minds in Congress that deprecated the policy of sending out letters-of-marque in this war with rebels; but the subject was much agitated, and in July 1862, Mr. Seward wrote to Mr. Adams, that he might inform Earl Russell "Since the Oreto and other gunboats are being received by the insurgents from Europe to renew demonstrations on our national commerce, Congress is about to authorize the issue of letters-of-marque and reprisal, and that if we find it necessary to suppress this piracy we shall bring privateers into service for that purpose and of course for that purpose only."

This was a qualified and harmless admonition which was duly appreciated by Earl Russell, particularly when he learned a few days after, that Congress had adjourned without taking action on the subject. In the meantime the depredations of the Alabama and Florida increased the irritation against not only the rebels but mercenary England.

On the 29th of September, Mr. Seward warned me that there were extensive combinations to break the blockade and to confirm his admonition, brought me a dispatch and documents from Mr. Dudley, our efficient consul at Liverpool. The dispatches were a notification that eight or ten steamers were nearly ready to run the blockade; but there was no evidence to confirm the apprehensions of the Secretary of State. No mention was made of any armed vessels, but there were reports of wonderful activity among the merchant adventurers of Great Britain, stimulated by the tidings of our disasters under Gen. Pope at Bull Run, which they had just previously received, and which they considered conclusive that the Union cause could not be sustained. Mr. Seward had mistaken unarmed English blockade runners for armed blockade breakers. Although relieved by my remarks he persisted still that the policy of letters-of-marque was advisable and proposed that the powerful merchant-steamer Baltic should be commissioned, and Comstock, a very competent merchant-captain, somewhat connected with, and used by the New York Ring should be placed in command. Such a proceeding on the part of the government would have been a reflection on naval officers and could not be entertained, there was yet no authority to grant letters-of-marque, and if the Baltic were chartered or purchased by the Navy, she must I assured him, be commanded by a naval officer.

So long as the subject remained under executive control the prudence and firmness of the President insured the national welfare and safety. But the public mind had become angry and highly inflamed, in which Congress participated, and on the 3rd of March 1863, the last day of the session, an Act was passed declaring, " that in all domestic and foreign wars the President
" of the United States is authorized to issue to private
" armed vessels of the United States, commissions or
" letters-of-marque and general reprisal in such form
" as he shall think proper, and under the seal of the
" United States, and make all needful rules and regu-
" lations for the government thereof, and for the adju-
" dication and disposal of the prizes and salvages made
" by each vessel—*provided* that the authority confer-
" red by this Act shall cease and terminate at the end
" of three years from the passage of this Act."

This action of Congress, though general in its character would, it was anticipated, have a favorable effect abroad. England would be admonished that there was a limit to American forbearance. Viewing it in this light, and as a warning to Great Britain where the spirit of unscrupulous greed, if not of positive enmity to the Union, had embarked an immense capital in schemes of illicit traffic in violation of our laws and of the blockade, the brief and modified enactment was acquiesced in. It was moreover felt, notwithstanding the favor which the project received from the Secretary of State, that the country would be secure against any rash or precipitate measure by the President to whom the whole subject was committed. But, unfortunately, the effect of the enactment, and the feeling which forced its passage, proved a stimulant which brought strength, and added unexpected recruits to the movement. Among others, the Secretary of the Treasury, on whom the more cautious and prudent had relied, became a convert to, or avowed advocate for, privateers and reprisals. The Secretary of State was much elated by the enactment, and by the acquisition of the Secretary of the Treasury to his policy. He also represented that merchants of New York were ready and anxious to fit out privateers to take the Alabama and Florida, and proposed at once to take measures for carrying the law into effect. But the President still hesitated, though the law, considered as an expression of the sentiment of the legislative branch of the government, together with the countenance which it received from the Secretary of the Treasury, who was understood to be the special representative and exponent of the commercial interest, had each an influence which it was difficult successfully to resist. I had from the first maintained that commerce being sensitive, intelligent merchants and capitalists would not engage in such enterprises—that privateers were usually excited by the expectation of large returns from captured merchantmen—that the Alabama and Florida, plundering rovers which they would, under present circumstances be commissioned to overtake, would, if captured, be found destitute of cargo or merchandize, and that vessels of sufficient magnitude and power to cope successfully with the Alabama would require a large investment for so uncertain a venture. Without naming persons, Mr, Seward insisted there were responsible parties ready to engage in the work so soon as they could be licensed, he therefore proceeded at once to prepare forms and make " needful rules and regulations" for the government of privateers in conformity with the recent Act. These regulations covering a number of pages, he, on the 10th of March, one week after the enactment submitted to me for review, criticism and suggestions. As I was wholly opposed to the proceeding, I declined the labor, admitted they conformed to the legal enactments of 1812; but in a free Cabinet discussion I made some general remarks, excepting to the regulations as transcending executive authority. The subject lingered for two or three weeks during a portion of which time I was absent from Washington and the President declined to come to a decision while I was away. Soon after my return, Mr. Seward brought forward the subject and said that parties interested were becoming impatient. He proposed that I should communicate my objections to his rules in writing, and the President concurred in the suggestion. I therefore in a day or two, addressed to him the following letter:

"Navy Department,
March 31st, 1863.
" Sir :—
" When discussing the regulations concerning 'letters-of-marque,' etc., a few days since, I made certain

suggestions, and you invited me to communicate any views I might entertain in writing.

"I have felt some delicacy, I may say disinclination, to take any active part in this matter, because I have from the beginning of our difficulties discouraged the policy of privateering in such a war as this we are now waging. The rebels have no commercial marine to entice and stimulate private enterprise and capital in such undertakings, provided the policy were desirable. We, however, have a commerce that invites the cupidity, zeal and spirit of adventure, which, once commenced, it will be difficult to regulate or suppress. A few privateers let loose among our shipping, like wolves among sheep would make sad havoc, as the Alabama and the Florida bear witness. It is proposed to encourage private enterprise to embark in an undertaking to capture the two wolves or privateers that are abroad devastating the seas; and it is said, in addition to the wolves, they may be authorized to catch blockade runners. The inducement, I apprehend will not meet a favorable response. There may be vessels fitted out to capture unarmed prizes, but not of sufficient force to meet and overcome the Alabama; if not, the great end and purpose of the scheme will fail of accomplishment.

"To clothe private armed vessels with governmental power and authority, including the belligerent right of search, will be likely to beget trouble, and the tendency must unavoidably be to abuse. Clothed with these powers, reckless men will be likely to involve the government in difficulty, and it was in apprehension of that fact, and to avoid it, I encountered much obloquy and reproach at the beginning of the rebellion, and labored to institute a less objectionable policy.

"Propositions for privateers, for yacht-squadrons, for naval brigades, volunteer navy, etc., etc., were, with the best intentions in most instances, pressed upon the department regardless of the consequences that might follow from these rude schemes of private warfare. It was to relieve us of the necessity of going into these schemes of private adventure, that the 'Act to provide for the temporary increase of the Navy,' approved July 24, 1861, was so framed as to give authority to take vessels into the naval service and to appoint officers for them, temporarily, to any extent which the President may deem expedient. Under other laws, seamen may be enlisted and their wages fixed by executive authority; and the officers and men so taken temporarily into the naval service are subject to the laws for the government of the navy. An 'Act for the better government of the navy, approved July 17, 1862, grants prize-money to any armed vessel in the service of the United States,' in the same manner as to vessels of the navy.

"These laws, therefore, seem and were intended to provide all the advantages of letters-of-marque, and yet prevent in a great measure, the abuses liable to spring from them. Private armed vessels, adopted temporarily into the naval service, would be more certainly and immediately under the control of the government, than if acting only under a general responsibility to law.

"It will be necessary to establish strict rules for the government of private armed vessels, as to some extent they will be likely to be officered and manned by persons of rude notions and free habits. Congress after authorizing letters-of-marque in the war of 1812, adopted the necessary legislation for the vessels bearing them, by the Act of June 26th of that year. This Act has not been revived. The recent Act concerning letters of-marque etc., etc., authorized the President to "make all needful rules and regulations for the government and conduct of private armed vessels, furnished with letters-of-marque.' In pursuance of this authorization, the 'Regulations' have been prepared, embracing the provisions of the statute enacted during the War of 1812. These regulations establish, as the statute did a penal code. They impose fines and assume to authorize punishments, including even capital punishment.

"As suggested in our interview, I question the validity of such proceedings. Can Congress delegate this power of penal legislation to the President? and if to the President, why may it not to any branch of the executive?

"If it can be granted for this special purpose—the government of private armed vessels—why not for any other purpose? And if it can delegate the power of penal legislation, why could it not delegate any other power or powers, to the President, to Commissioners, or even to a Committee of its own body, to sit during the recess? Why could it not delegate authority to the Secretary of the Treasury to legislate respecting imports, foreign trade, or to the Postmaster-general full power of legislation respecting postoffices and post routes? The power of imposing penalties and inflicting punishments is the essence of legislative power, for it is the penalty of transgression that gives force to law. These regulations also establish rewards as well as penalties. They provide that a large bounty shall be paid to private armed vessels in certain cases. But no fund is appropriated for the purpose by the Act, nor has any provision elsewhere been made for it. Can Congress delegate to the President the power to appropriate the public moneys, or to take them without specific appropriation, or pledge the public faith at his discretion for an indefinite amount?

"As I have already said I have doubts in these particulars. They are expressed with some reluctance, because in the uneasy condition of the public mind, growing out of the lawless depredations of the semi-piratical cruisers that are abroad, I am unwilling to interpose anything which may be construed into an obstacle to repress public indignation, which is so justly excited. I did not regret that Congress enacted a law authorizing letters-of-marque; because I verily believe that, with it, England can be made to prevent her mercenary citizens from making war on our commerce under a flag that has no recognized nationality. If the police of the sea is to be surrendered, and rovers built by English capital and manned by Englishmen are to be let loose to plunder our commerce, let England understand that her ships will suffer, and her commerce also be annoyed and injured by private armed ships. With her distant and dependent colonies, no nation has greater cause to oppose maritime robbery and plunder, such as is being inflicted on us by Englishmen and English capital, than Great Britain.

"The West Indies are, notoriously, harbors of refuge for the cruisers that are plundering our merchants, as well as for the infamous and demoralizing business of running our blockade, to encourage the insurgents who are waging war on our government. Of these ports, those of England are the worst, and a vast amount of English capital is engaged in illicit traffic, and her people and authorities exhibit sympathy for and afford aid to the insurgents and their abettors, and corresponding opposition to this government.

"The English ship-yards are filled with vessels built and building for the rebel service, and if measures are not taken to prevent, these will soon swarm the seas to capture, condemn and destroy American property, without a port into which they can send their captures for adjudication. Enjoying greater advantages than the corsairs and sea-rovers that once infested the ocean, because protected, harbored and sheltered by governments in alliance with and professedly friendly to us, while ordinary pirates are outlaws, this species of lawless outrage cannot be permitted to go on.

"England should be warned that we cannot permit this indirect war to continue with impunity—that it will provoke and justify retaliation, and that if her people and government make war upon our commerce, by sending abroad rovers with no nationality, to prey upon the property of our citizens, it will be impossible to restrain our people from retaliatory measures.

"I am respectfully,
"Your ob'd't serv't,
"GIDEON WELLES,
"*Sec't'y of Navy.*"
"HON. WM. H. SEWARD,
"*Sec't'y of State.*"

Whilst this letter was on my table, Senator Sumner, who had opposed the law when on its passage, called on me, and was very much disturbed by what he had learned from Mr. Seward would be the probable policy of the administration. From the commencement he had objected to licensing privateers, and was, when he called, a good deal incensed at some remarks of the Secretary of State whom he had just left. It was felt by Mr. Seward to be something of a triumph over Mr. Sumner, who often came in conflict with his views, and in allusion to whom, when confronted, as he sometimes was by the President with the Senator's opinions, he remarked, "there were too many Secretaries of State in Washington." I handed to Mr. Sumner during the interview, my letter which was yet unsent, to read, and remarked as I did so, that I was very much disappointed at the recent course of Mr. Chase, and discouraged by communications just received from Earl Russell. He expressed great gratification with my letter, but hoped before I sent it to the State Department that I would read it to Mr. Lincoln; this was not my practice. I could not doubt that Mr. Seward himself on its receipt would submit it to the President.

The evening after this interview, the President came across the Square to my house, which was directly opposite the executive mansion, and said his principal object in calling was to see a letter I had prepared, which Mr. Sumner had read and complimented, and wished him to peruse. I informed him that the letter had gone to Mr. Seward, but I would bring him the press copy in the morning. He thought this unnecessary for Mr. Seward would undoubtedly present it. He then discussed this subject with others at considerable length. The President met my disbelief that merchants of character and intelligence would be induced to engage in the business of privateering, and my opinion that Mr. Seward was deceiving himself in that respect, by asking whether the best method of testing the fact would not be by giving the merchants an opportunity to manifest their views by their acts. Let us see, said he, who the men are that are ready and anxious to aid the government in this way; perhaps you are mistaken and Seward right. Chase who knows, or ought to know the commercial sentiment has come into Seward's views. It may be well to make the experiment. The State and the Treasury may know more correctly the feelings of the merchants than the Navy. I replied, the test would be hazardous. Should the merchants, as Mr. Seward believed, embark in the measure, adventurers would be likely to also engage in reprisals, and might involve us in war which with the load upon our hands would be disastrous. We ought therefore to act deliberately, and with a full and right appreciation of all the probable consequences. He said that was true and he had confidence in my judgment and my opinions, but I might be mistaken—the State and the Treasury took a different view, and if I was right in my belief that the merchants would not engage in privateering, no harm could come from the trial. If Seward was mistaken, and the substantial men of the country held off, the credit would be mine, and all would then be satisfied.

At the Cabinet meeting on Friday the 3d of April Mr. Seward had some side talk with me in relation to the assignment of a naval officer of character to the service of the State Department, on whom he could devolve the labor and details of examining applications and preparing papers. He had previously requested that Admiral Foote should be detailed for that service, but that officer after looking into the subject requested to be excused. As all matters relating to privateers and letters-of-marque had in former wars been committed to the State Department and were to be on this occasion, I objected that the navy ought not to be blended with the movement. He very frankly said his purpose in asking for a naval officer of rank, was to be relieved himself of labor and details—in other words, I perceived the Navy Department was to share in the responsibility of any failure or imbroglio that might result from a policy which it disapproved. He named Rear-Admiral C. H. Davis as acceptable, who was assigned accordingly.

The President requested to see me on the following morning, Saturday, and as I entered the room he remarked that I would probably be surprised to hear that Seward already had application for letters-of-marque. I acknowledged I was disappointed if there were respectable and responsible parties to engage in the business. The President said he knew nothing of the gentleman whom Seward had brought him, farther than that he had a vessel, and was anxious to enter upon the service. Taking up and looking at a paper, he said the gentleman's name was Seybert, that he had a vessel of one hundred tons, into which he proposed to put a screw—that this gentleman was then in the audience room, and he would call him in, that I might examine him. This I informed him was unnecessary, for I was familiar with the case which had already been before me. There were, I assured the President no New York merchants or capital in this enterprise. Seybert was, I had learned, a Prussian adventurer, who called himself a citizen of South Carolina, and I preferred that the Secretary of State should dispose of this and all other similar applications. With a twinkle in his eye the President said he certainly would not trouble me farther in this instance, but wait for the merchants.

Senator Sumner informed me at the same time that the President had experienced great difficulty in getting a sight of my letter of the 31st of March. Mr. Seward did not bring it to his notice as was expected, and when he asked for it, one excuse after another was given, but the President persisted until it was sent him, when he notified the Senator, and together they read it, and discussed the whole subject of privateering and reprisals.

This, with Seybert's application, the only one that ever after came to my knowledge, terminated the privateer policy, closed the subject of letters-of-marque and reprisals during the rebellion. I never again saw the Regulations or heard them alluded to. That Mr. Seward was earnest and sincere in his belief that privateers might render efficient service, I never questioned, but it was fortunate for the administration and the country, that he did not direct affairs for the nation in regard to the policy of letters-of-marque during our civil war. Mr. Lincoln proved himself on that subject and others through that whole exciting period, the "superior in native intellectual power," and in administrative ability.

OFFICIAL intercourse between the Secretary of State, and the Secretary of the Navy was probably more frequent than between any other two departments. The service of naval officers on foreign stations where courtesy and the obligations of treaties were to be observed and maintained, and questions growing out of the exercise of belligerent rights, including those of blockade, contraband and the right of search, brought the heads of these two departments in contact, and rendered consultations necessary. These consultations, often in personal interviews, but sometimes by correspondence, brought out the points in which they agreed and disagreed, developed the views of each and to some extent the policy and principles and the working of the administration. But however antagonistic their opinions, there was between the two Secretaries always harmony and mutual good-will and friendly personal relations during the years they were associated together. When they did not agree on any public measure, the subject was submitted to the President who usually decided for himself; but sometimes the differences were made the subject of Cabinet consultation. As a general thing the Secretary of State was averse to bringing department differences before the Cabinet. Visiting the President daily, there were occasions when Mr. Seward obtained a decision without the President's being aware of any difference, or that the point was contested. A decision once made and promulgated it was often difficult to have it reversed. In mentioning these and other incidents rendered necessary in remarking on the " Memorial Address," my object has been to exhibit the executive ability and peculiar management of Mr. Seward, which Mr. Adams assumes, and many have believed, controlled and directed the administration of Mr. Lincoln. Such was not the fact. The ideas of the two as to the extent and exercise of executive authority were different, the grants and limitations of power by the constitution were less respected by the Secretary of State than by the President, hence Mr. Seward often and especially when Congress was not in session, freely and sometimes inconsiderately if not rashly, gave unfortunate opinions—conceded away important rights, and himself, exercised questionable executive authority, on the assumption, apparently, that the executive was the government, and his power in the administration almost absolute. Nevertheless Mr. Seward was timid in facing Congress, felt his responsibility to the legislative department more than to the Constitution and disliked controversy, especially with associates who were compelled to sometimes question the correctness of his views. His readiness to manifest his authority and magnify his position led him to make off-hand promises and to decide questions without first investigating and ascertaining their true merits, or his authority to act and his power to fulfil his engagements. This precipitancy not unfrequently begat embarassment and betrayed not only a want of wise diplomatic reserve, but of calm and intelligent executive ability. But if he was at times rash and arbitrary it was from personal weakness, a desire to show his power rather than from malevolence or want of patrioitsm. Towards the demands of foreign governments, particularly the great powers who were often wrong and unreasonable. he was submissive, too ready to yield and make concessions that could not be justified, and which were in fact sometimes a surrender of undoubted national rights.

In October 1862, Mr. Seward sent me the copy of a singular letter from the Spanish Minister claiming that the dominion of Spain extended six miles instead of three from the coast of Cuba. In his reception and treatment of this absurd demand, and in transmitting the letter making the claim, Mr. Seward unwittingly erred and made some unfortunate admissions, said "the questions raised were important and by no means easy of solution"—yet there was no principle or rule better settled by the consent and practice of maritime nations, than that the marine league or three miles off the open sea was the extent of sovereign dominion. This novel assumption if permitted or entertained would have been a wonderful protection to the rebels and blockade-runners that were swarming the waters of Cuba and its vicinity. Instead of squarely meeting and promptly dismissing this strange claim made at a strange period, when we were engaged in a deadly struggle with the insurgents and their covert allies, or bringing the subject before the Cabinet, Mr. Seward had allowed himself to discuss it. Instead of appealing to the law of nations which no Secretary of State could change, he had, sitting in the State Department, incautiously and improperly put our rights in jeopardy by admitting that the Spanish government, when it asserted that an improvement in ordnance enlarged the marine jurisdiction of every sovereign, had "set forth a true principle of international law." But the law should have governed him. Neither he nor the Spainish Minister, nor both combined could revoke it. Other nations were interested. He might as he had undertaken in the matter of the captured mails, renounce the right of the United States, but that would not unsettle or change the law of nations. The following is the correspondence referred to:

"DEPARTMENT OF STATE.
"Washington, Oct. 10, 1862.
"SIR: —
"I have the honor to communicate for your information, a copy of a note which has been received at this Department from His Excellency Señor Don Gabriel Garcia y Tassara, Minister-Plenipotentiary of Her Catholic Majesty, on the subject of the marine dominion appurtenant to the island of Cuba. You will learn from this paper that Spain claims that this dominion covers six miles upon the open sea, instead of three miles as it has been understood by this government. The questions raised by this note are important, and by no means easy of solution. The Spanish Government sets forth a true principle of international law when it states that the marine jurisdiction of every sovereign extends the length of a cannon shot from the shore. It has however, been generally agreed, by the acquiescence rather than by the formal consent of nations, that this extent is a marine league, or three miles. Spain now claims that the limit may be extended beyond the three miles, so however, as to be kept within the length of a gun-shot, as it is extended by modern improvements in the machinery of ordnance, and that each nation may fix the limit of its

own marine dominion, with that reservation, for itself, without making general or specific arrangements for the purpose with other states. Spain, moreover, claims that she has thus fixed the limit for herself at six miles. The subject will receive due examination by this Department. As a preliminary to that examination, I have the honor to ask you how the allowance of this claim would practically effect the efficiency of the navy in the exercise of such belligerent rights as the United States have occasion to maintain and exercise in the vicinity of Cuba.

"I am, Sir, Your Ob't Serv't,
"WM H. SEWARD."
"Hon. Gideon Welles,
"*Sec't'y of the Navy.*"

"NAVY DEPARTMENT,
"SIR:— Oct. 15, 1862.
"I have the honor to acknowledge the receipt of your communication of the 10th inst. covering the dispatch of His Excellency Don G. G. Tassara, Minister-Plenipotentiary of Her Catholic Majesty, on the subject of the marine dominion appurtenant to the island of Cuba—claiming that it covers six miles upon the open sea, instead of three miles as hitherto understood by this government—admitting the recognized principle that marine jurisdiction extends to cannon ball range, and citing modern improvements in artillery as authority in support of his claim.

"You do me the honor to ask me, as preliminary to the examination which you propose to make, how the allowance of this claim would practically affect the efficiency of the Navy in the exercise of such belligerent rights as the United States have occasion to maintain and exercise in the vicinity of Cuba."

"The concession of this claim would be inconsistent with the exercise of our belligerent rights at this juncture, in consequence of the constant and flagrant abuse of neutral flags by a class of contrabandists who make it their business to set our laws at defiance, violate our blockade and aid and assist the insurgents in the war which they are waging upon our government. The vessels engaged in this system of indirect aggression upon a country at peace with Spain, when pursued by our cruisers, fly to the shelter of neutral territory to escape, and the more extended the maritime jurisdiction of Cuba and the possessions of other governments in the West Indies, the greater impunity to these violators of our laws.

"We have no wish to intrude upon the unquestioned rights of Spain, whose government has manifested a friendly spirit and just regard towards us in other particulars, but the assertion of this extended jurisdiction at this particular period, I should deem unfortunate. The effect would be to aid and encourage mischievous wrong-doers and to inflict injury upon a friendly nation in the day of her misfortune.

"At a more propitious moment, the question of maritime jurisdiction and the influence of modern improvement in ordnance upon it, might be discussed and settled with advantage; but the present time is inopportune for such a novel interpretation of the law of nations. The publicists and the world generally have hitherto regarded the marine league adjacent to the coast as the limit of territorial jurisdiction, and our Naval officers in this particular have concurred in this view.

"Permit me to add that the object of law is to put an end to license and discretion and to establish a fixed rule which all may ascertain, and be guided by. It is a provision of international law that the jurisdiction of a state extends to a marine league or cannon range, beyond its shores. The marine league is something fixed and definite; the cannon range is not. To insist on excluding the former and retaining the latter only, would be to revive the license and uncertainty which it was the purpose of the law to prevent. The question and dispute would be constantly recurring. What is the range of a cannon?

"There is no doubt that the marine league was adopted because it was near, but somewhat more than the extreme range of the heaviest ordnance in ordinary use, when the rule was adopted; and it is so now, notwithstanding the improvements in ordnance. Cannon range is merely referred to in the rule as showing the reason of the rule; if it had been intended to be the rule in itself, it would have been absurd to refer at the same time to the marine league. The marine league is now universally regarded as the fixed rule.

"If ordnance should come into general use, throwing their projectiles to a greater distance than a league, nations might feel called upon to consult with each other as to a revision of the rule. But in the meantime for any one nation to repudiate it, is simply to set itself above the obligation of international law, without even the pretence of necessity. What real danger or inconvenience is apprehended from a continuance of the rule?

"I am respectfully,
"Your Ob't. Servt.,
"GIDEON WELLES,
"*Sec'ty of Navy.*"

"HON. WM. H. SEWARD,
Sec'ty of State."

Unfortunately the Secretary had said too much to the Spanish diplomat to retract, and put himself in a right position, without a virtual acknowledgment of error in the early discussion; and the Minister was not inclined to relinquish the ground he had gained, but continued to press his advantage. The result was, that instead of referring to and abiding by the law and by established usage and practice, the Secretary and the Minister agreed to submit the question to the king of the Belgians for a decision, and the project for a Convention for that purpose was drawn up by which the two governments stipulated in the second article, to " abide by the decision of His said Majesty."

When, more than a year after this arrangement between the two functionaries, had been entered into, though not confirmed by the Senate, I learned what was proposed to be done, I objected that the consent to submit our unquestioned and undoubted right to arbitration was wrong. There was little doubt the decision would, as Mr. Seward felt confident, be favorable to us in conformity to the law and the practice of nations, but it was highly improper and not good and faithful administration to put our undoubted rights in jeopardy. Had Spain laid claim to the possession of Long Island or Nantucket, the idea of submitting the claim to the decision of the king of the Belgians or any other king would never have been for a moment entertained. Nor should the principle and our legal right in regard to the great highway of nations which Spain had undertaken to invade and appropriate to her exclusive jurisdiction, be matter of arbitrament, nor would other governments, whatever might be the decision regard it as obligatory on them.

Mr. Adams says, "in respect to the foreign relations, Mr. Lincoln knew absolutely nothing," but that "it may be questioned whether any head of an executive department ever approached Mr. Seward in the extent and minuteness of the instructions he was constantly issuing during the critical period of the war." These frequent and minute instructions and concessions, incautiously given and admitted, were often erroneous and embarrassing. Had the preposterous pretensions of the Spanish Minister which Mr. Seward listened to and consented to negotiate been successful, scarcely a greater or more injurious error could be found in our history. It would have afforded great additional security to the rebels and blockade-runners.

SIMULTANEOUSLY with this Spanish claim of an extension of maritime jurisdiction the Secretary of State sent me a copy of an unofficial note from Mr. Stuart of the English legation, and at the time, Charge d'affaires, expressing apprehensions that the "Bermuda," a captured blockade-runner would be purchased by the Navy Department and taken into service prior to condemnation. We were at that time availing ourselves of every suitable steamer in the country that could be armed and made efficient in enforcing our extensive blockade, which Earl Russell had pronounced at the beginning of our troubles an impossibility; but in due time he admitted it was effective. When the blockade was first proclaimed we could neither build, nor buy from our merchant service a sufficient number of vessels to enforce it and therefore had a standing order to obtain from the courts, such prizes as were in the possession of the prize-commissioners and liable to condemnation. In this way we procured many excellent steamers, which having been built for speed were a valuable acquisition to our naval force. This proceeding became a great annoyance to our open enemies, and no less so to their secret allies who were largely engaged in illicit traffic, and found their risks increased by some of their own most valuable and expensive vessels which were turned against them. To prevent this as far as possible, and if they could not wholly prevent, to postpone as long as possible the condemnation of the steamers captured, delays in court were interposed and the legality of the captures contested, although there was not a doubt that they would ultimately be condemned as good prize. In the meantime the prizes were, besides the detention, deteriorating and often in a perishing condition. The courts and prize-commissioners acting in good faith to both captors and claimants, always had vessel and cargo promptly appraised and disposed of at their true value, and the money paid into court to abide the final decree. That there might be no delay in the transfer, a board consisting of a naval constructor, engineer and ordnance officer was empowered by the Secretary of the Navy to make a thorough examination of every prize deemed suitable for naval service, and on a favorable report he deposited the amount of the appraised value with the registrar of the court, and had her immediately taken to the Navy-yard, fitted and armed for naval duty.

This was the state of facts and the course of proceeding when Mr. Stuart, Her Majesty's Charge d'affaires on the 20th of October, 1862 sent his note, shrewdly made *unofficial*, to Mr. Seward, Secretary of State. The latter without knowledge of the facts, and without investigation or inquiry—without consulting the President or Cabinet or any one of them, committed himself at once against the Navy Department and the government, and in an *official* communication "*hoped* the unofficial apprehensions of Mr. Stuart are unfounded, as such a measure would afford ground for serious complaint on the part of the British government, which under existing circumstances it is desirable to avoid."

It was a timid and hasty abandonment of a right, an admission of wrong on our part, and an acknowledgement of the propriety of foreign interference, wholly unjustifiable, aside from the obvious intent of keeping out of our service as long as possible an important prize, captured in its attempts to supply the insurgents with munitions of war.

Subjoined is the correspondence:

"DEPARTMENT OF STATE,
WASHINGTON, Oct. 10, 1862."

"SIR:—

"I have the honor to enclose a copy of an unofficial note of this date, addressed to me by Mr. Stuart, Her Britannic Majesty's Charge d'affaires, expressing apprehensions that the steamer "Bermuda" may be taken for the use of the Navy Department prior to her condemnation at Philadelphia. It is to be hoped that these apprehensions are unfounded as such a measure would afford ground for serious complaint on the part of the British Government, which under existing circumstances, it is desirable to avoid.

"I have the honor to be, &c,
"WM. H. SEWARD."
"THE HON. GIDEON WELLES,
"Sec't'y of the Navy."

"NAVY DEPARTMENT,
Oct. 15, 1862."
"SIR :—

"I had the honor on the evening of Saturday last, the 11th inst. to receive your communication of the 10th inst. enclosing the copy of an unofficial note from Mr. Stuart, Her Britannic Majesty's Charge d'affaires, expressing an apprehension that it is the intention of the naval authorities to appropriate the steamer Bermuda, although no judgment has as yet been pronounced upon her by the court.

"This is certainly a very extraordinary communication from Her Majesty's Charge d'affaires. The custody of captured property, or the disposition to be made of it before adjudication, is not regulated by international law, but that law requires that an adjudication should be had as speedily as possible.

"In some cases the captors themselves have a right to dispose of captured property before adjudication. (2. Rob. 31.)

"The court, after the captured property comes into its possession, may deliver it on bond to the captors or claimants, or if ship or other cargo is in a perishing condition or liable to deterioration pending the process, may order a sale of it by interlocutory decree. This is the English law and the practice followed by our courts. There is no doubt as to this discretionary power of a prize-court or as to the practice. The property is always supposed to be in the custody of the court, but the practice has been from time immemorial to consider the proceeds as representing the thing itself. Certainly the safest custodian of the property is the government, which is ultimately responsible. The marshal, who ordinarily has the custody, is but an officer of the government. In the event of a decree of restitution, if the custodian has been found to be unfaithful and the captors unable to indemnify the foreign claimants, the government must make the restitution and indemnify the claimants. There could be no additional risk to the claimants, but rather the contrary, if the government should take immediate possession of the captured property without waiting an order of the prize-court. All that international law requires is, that the evidence and all the necessary witnesses be placed in the presence of the court.

"International law is rigid against individual captors; they should not pillage in the slightest degree, upon pain of forfeiting their rights. But it does not pretend to lay down rules for the custody of captured property. It is enough that the government of the captors is ultimately responsible for any injury done by the captors.

"The Bermuda was captured on the 27th of April, 1862, about fifteen miles N. E. by E. from the "Hole in the Wall," and brought into Philadelphia. She has been appraised by order of the court, on application of the prize-commissioners, and the Navy Department proposes to purchase her under the decree of the court. If so, the amount of valuation will be deposited in conformity with law and the order of the court with the registrar. The whole proceeding is strictly legal and strictly regular and for the benefit of all having a legal interest in the captured steamer.

"There is no novelty in these proceedings. Other captured vessels have in like manner been disposed of, and not infrequently purchased by the Navy Department on appraisement, not only in Philadelphia under the order of Judge Cadwalader, but in New York under Judge Betts, and in Key West under Judge Marvin. But these are matters in which I recognize no right for foreign interference. The capture was lawful and *prima facie* correct.

"It was made under the authority of the United States in the exercise of an undoubted belligerent right. But the capture is subject to adjudication, and if the court shall fail to condemn, the United States must and will respond in damages. But until the final judgment of the court, I know of no right for foreign interference.

"I cannot forbear the expression of my surprise at the interposition of Her Majesty's representative in behalf of a vessel captured with such an amount of contraband of war on board intended to afford assistance to rebels who are waging war upon this government. Her cargo of guns, shot, shell, powder, etc., is a perfect magazine of munitions designed, as you and I well knew before she left the shores of England, for those of our countrymen who are in insurrection. Taken as she was on the high seas with contraband of war on board in large quantities, does Her Majesty's representative appear, *even unofficially*, in behalf of this vessel, whose mission was to do wrong—to violate our laws, injure our country and furnish insurgent rebels with the means to destroy our countrymen, with whom he and his government are professedly on terms of amity and friendship ?

" Assuredly Her Majesty's Charge d'affaires could not have been aware of the character of the steamer Bermuda and her cargo, or he would never have permitted himself to have been interested for her. Captured as she was on the high seas, filled with material to inflict wrong upon a nation with which Great Britain is at peace, I confess my astonishment at the interposition of Her Majesty's Charge d'affaires in the action of our courts. The case of the Bermuda is so transparently wrong as to admit of no doubt as to the final result in regard to her, but were it otherwise, the government of the United States is not only abundantly able to respond, but is always anxious to do right in matters of this description. We may be wronged and experience bad faith from others, but these will never induce our courts or our government to be unjust.

" The opportunity is not an improper one for me to invite your attention to the conduct of the British Colonial authorities in permitting Her Majesty's Proclamation to be constantly disregarded, and good faith and the laws of neutrality to be persistently violated. Vessels, as is known to us and to the whole world, are constantly leaving certain ports in the British West Indies, avowedly to run our blockade and furnish assistance to the insurgents in their criminal assault upon our government. Nassau is notoriously an *entrepôt* for systematic arrangements to violate our blockade, where cargoes are interchanged, contraband of war transhipped, and vessels are received and fitted out, despite the remonstrance of our Consul, who has repeatedly brought these flagitious proceedings to the notice of the public authorities. So flagrant indeed was the case of the

Oreto that she was once or twice detained, and after the formality of a trial, most extraordinary in its character and results, was permitted to depart by the British Courts, and, as is well known, directly after, ran the blockade at Mobile.

"But the Colonial authorities are not alone in fault. More recently we have intelligence that the steamer '290' *alias* the 'Alabama,' which our Consul and our Minister at London warned the British authorities was being prepared to depredate upon our commerce and make war upon our flag, but which in spite of these remonstrances they permitted to escape, has got abroad and is seizing, sinking and burning the property of innocent merchants.

"Who is to be responsible for the devastation made by this rebel rover which has never yet visited the ports of any other country but those of Great Britain, when the government of that country was repeatedly admonished of her true character and purpose before she left its shores?

"I know of no case in history that has a parallel in the enormity of the outrage committed, as between friendly nations, to that of this semi-piratical vessel from England which is now plundering and destroying our commerce. From the commencement of the insurrection, the insurgents who are making war upon our government and endeavoring to subvert it, without a naval vessel of their own afloat or a port free of access, have gone to England—a power that is professedly on terms of amity with the United States—and there have experienced no difficulty in contracting for and procuring to be built and sent forth, a cruiser, armed* and ladened with munitions of war, to make waste and destruction with the property of our citizens who are wholly uninformed, and consequently wholly unprepared for such aggressive proceedings under any guise from Great Britain. This vessel which is committing these outrages upon peaceful commerce, it will be borne in mind, has never visited the waters of any nation but those of Great Britain, is committing havoc upon the commerce of a people who enjoyed, as they supposed, peaceful relations with that country.

"On every principle of equity and right, morally and politically, the British nation should be held responsible for the losses which our citizens sustain by the depredations which this semi-piratical cruiser, which was built on British soil, and went forth from a British port against the remonstrance and protests of our Minister and Consul, to prey upon American commerce.

"I do not permit myself to doubt that you have been attentive to these facts and have duly presented them in the proper quarter, asserting our rights and our sense of the injury that our country and countrymen have received. But I have deemed it not inopportune, nor improper in me, to invite your especial attention to the subject, because there is no concealment of the fact that there are at this time vessels being built and others purchased and fitted out with arms and munitions and contraband of war in various places in Great Britain, notoriously to promote aggressive war against the United States.

"I am respectfully,
"Your obed't serv't,
"GIDEON WELLES,
"*Sec'ty of the Navy.*"

"HON. WM. H. SEWARD,
"*Sec'ty of State.*"

This correspondence, it will be noticed, was not

with Lord Lyons, the Minister, who was then absent, but with Mr. Stuart a subordinate then temporarily in charge of the legation, and who improved his opportunity, which Lord Lyons would scarcely have asked to obtain concessions from our Secretary of State in the case of captured mails as well as captured vessels. In the case of captured mails, it will be remembered Lord Lyons disavowed to Mr. Sumner that he had ever made a demand, but that it was a voluntary renunciation of our right by our Secretary of State who was supposed to be the authorized organ of the government. In a letter of the 31st of December following, Lord Lyons, who had resumed his duties, admitted that by "a British statute authorizing the sale of a ship before the decision of an appellate court has been pronounced, is well-founded,"—that "the exercise of such an abstract power of sale is not denied by Her Majesty's Government to the United States authorities," but, he thought "the claimant ought to be preferred as a purchaser," etc.

This letter of the British Minister disposed of the unofficial apprehensions of his subordinate—apprehensions in which the Secretary of State participated, and "hoped were unfounded," but which the Secretary of the Navy, thus admonished or rebuked, disregarded. The transfer in this and other cases, was carried into effect, notwithstanding hopes and fears and timid concessions of the experienced government official, who according to Mr. Adams, had the "solid power to direct affairs"—and possessed "breadth of philosophic experience" and "native intellectual power" greatly superior to Mr. Lincoln.

The President had a happy way of illustrating questions and sometimes disposing of a subject by an anecdote, which, better than an elaborate argument, expressed his opinion. In the latter part of the winter of 1864, Mr. Seward came one day to the cabinet council with a full portfolio, and brow clouded and disturbed. The President ever watchful, immediately detected difficulty, and exhibited his concern as the Secretary of State slowly adjusted his papers. Mr. Seward commenced by alluding to the fact that Spain was sick of the European alliance, and was beginning to manifest towards our country a more friendly spirit; that her government had never been fully identified with Palmerston and Louis Napoleon in their intrigue for European intervention, but she had at the beginning of American troubles committed herself to some extent and been induced to undertake to recover her possessions in San Domingo. She had however been unfortunate and met unexpected resistance. The negroes were making a great struggle to maintain their independence, and had the sympathies of the abolitionists of our country with them. It was important in every point of view to detach Spain from the alliance and preserve her friendship, at the same time not give offence to our own countrymen whose sympathies in the present condition of affairs were enlisted in behalf of the negroes. In this Spanish-Dominican complication we were pressed from both quarters, and it was a delicate and grave question what position we should take and what course pursue. On one side was Spain, whom we wish to conciliate, on the other side, the negroes who had become great favorites and wanted our good-will in resisting Spanish oppression.

The President's countenance indicated that his mind was relieved before Seward had concluded. He remarked that the dilemma of the Secretary of State reminded him of an interview between two negroes in Tennessee. One was a preacher, who with the crude and strange notions of the ignorant of his race was endeavoring to admonish and enlighten his brother African of the importance of religion and the dangers of the future. " Dere are," said Josh, the preacher, " two roads before you, Jo. Be careful which you take. One ob dem roads leads straight to hell—de odder goes right to damnation." Jo opened his eyes with affright and under the inspired eloquence, and awful danger before him exclaimed, " Josh, take which road you please—I shall go thro' de woods."

" I am not willing," said the President, " to assume any new troubles or responsibility at this time, and shall therefore avoid going to one place with Spain or with the negro to the other, but shall take to the woods. We will maintain an honest and strict neutrality."

The relation of the circumstances attending the capture and release of the rebel emissaries, Mason and Slidell, is pregnant with error. The excitement which accompanied the intelligence of the capture of these mischievous men was great, and had at one time a threatening aspect. The final disposition of the question, with the restoration of the prisoners to British authority, might well be mentioned as displaying the marked and in some respects perhaps happy trait of Mr. Seward in adapting himself to circumstances which he could not control. But Mr. Adams fails to bring out that shrewd diplomatic quality of Mr. Seward's mind, and strives to inculcate an impression that the Secretary of State stood alone; was wise, sagacious, reserved, and profound, when others were blind, precipitate, and weak; took upon himself "the whole weight of popular indignation," and, "like the Roman Curtius, who leaped into the abyss which could have been closed in no other way," he offered himself a sacrifice to secure the safety of the state. Mr. Seward should receive credit for the dexterous and skilful dispatch which he prepared on his own change of position. It exhibits his readiness and peculiar tact and talent to extricate himself from and to pass over difficulties. But in point of fact no man was more elated or jubilant over the capture of the emissaries than Mr. Seward, who for a time made no attempt to conceal his gratification and approval of the act of Wilkes. But while he and most of the Cabinet and country were hilarious, the President had doubts, misgivings, and regrets, which were increased after an interview with Senator Sumner, with whom he often—sometimes to the disgust and annoyance of Mr. Seward—advised on controverted or disputed international questions, and especially when there were differences between himself and the Secretary of State.

On the question of giving up the emissaries, Mr. Adams says: "When the time came for the assembly of the Cabinet, not a sign had been given by the President, or any of the members, favorable to concession. Mr. Seward, who had been charged with the official duty of furnishing the expected answer, assumed the responsibility of preparing his able argument, upon which a decision was made to surrender the men. Upon him would have rested the whole weight of popular indignation had it proved formidable. If I have been rightly informed, when read, it met with few comments and less approbation. On the other hand, there was no resistance. Silence gave consent. It was the act of Mr. Seward, and his name was to be associated with it, whether for good or for evil."

The truth is, not only had the President expressed his doubts of the legality of the capture, and had them increased, while Mr. Seward was rejoicing over and approving of the proceeding, but Mr. Blair from the first had denounced the act as unathorized, irregular, and illegal. Not being a special admirer of Wilkes, Mr. Blair recommended that Wilkes should be ordered to take the Iroquois and go with Mason and Slidell to England, and deliver them to the British government; for Palmerston and Russell would, he said, seize the occasion to make war. The prompt and voluntary disavowal of the act of Wilkes, and delivering over the prisoners, would have evinced our confidence in our own power, and been a manifestation of our indifference and contempt for the emissaries, and a rebuke to the alleged intrigues between the rebels and the English Cabinet. Mr. Seward took a totally different view; scouted the idea of letting the prisoners go; said the British did not want them, and we could not think of delivering them up. While Mr. Blair did not go about at the time proclaiming his opinions on a subject which was under consideration, his dissent from the original views of the Secretary of State, and his condemnation of the act of Wilkes, are notorious among those who were intimate with the transactions of the government. The time for further withholding the facts, and permitting men like Mr. Adams to be misled, has gone by. The truth in relation to these and other matters, so long perverted and suppressed, should be known, and history set right.

Nearly every member of the administration, like Mr. Seward, rejoiced in the capture of these mischievous men. No one coincided with Mr. Blair in his suggestion to compel Wilkes to return them to the custody of Great Britain, however wise it may have been in view of subsequent events. But the irregular action of Wilkes in this case was in various ways the cause of serious embarrassment. If the proceedings could not be fully justified, neither could they, in the then condition of affairs, and the excited state of public feeling, be censured and condemned. But the Secretary of the Navy, before hearing from Great Britain, before even the administration had passed upon the subject, was compelled to recognize and approve or disapprove the act, and communicate the transaction in his Annual Navy Report, just then to be submitted to the President and Congress. In that Report, and in a congratulatory letter of the 30th of November, allusion is made to the irregularity of Wilkes, which, it is suggested, might be excused in view of the patriotic motives; "but it must by no means be permitted to constitute a precedent hereafter for the treatment of any similar infraction of neutral obligations by foreign vessels engaged in commerce or the carrying trade." This Report, though bearing date of the 2d of December, the day on which Congress convened, was, as is usual with Annual Reports, delivered complete to the President at the last regular Cabinet meeting preceding the session, which was on Friday, the 29th of November, 1861, to be transmitted with the Message. Of course the Naval Report was seen on that day by Mr. Seward, who until then had taken no exception to the capture; but on the succeeding day, the 30th of November, the date of the congratulatory letter to Wilkes, he wrote to Mr. Adams what the latter gentleman calls the "preliminary dispatch that saved the dignity of the country."

These matters, it will be borne in mind, were weeks before hearing from England, and before Mr. Seward's elaborate answer of the 26th of December to the demand of the British government for the surrender of the emissaries. When Mr. Adams declares that "not a sign had been given by the President or any member of the Cabinet favorable to concession," at the time that answer was prepared, he commits an egregious mistake. The President was from the first willing to make concession. Mr. Blair advocated it. Mr. Seward was at the beginning opposed to any idea of concession which involved giving up the emissaries, but yielded at once, and with dexterity, to the peremptory demand of Great Britain. Let him have all the applause which belongs to him for the facility and diplomatic skill which he displayed in that change, but in doing so, it is unjust to the President and others to misrepresent them, or to mistake or pervert the facts in regard to them or Mr. Seward.

THESE incidents selected from among many indicate something of the managing expediency, fertility of resources, and administrative manner of Mr. Seward, and illustrate the "superior intellectual power" and "force of moral discipline' which the "Memorial Address" undertakes to say, enabled him to "direct affairs for the benefit of the nation, through the name of another." Acting at times from impulse, often without sufficient forethought of consequences—fond of displaying power—frequently exercising questionable authority—prompted in some degree by jobbing and lobby surroundings which, fostered at Albany and defeated at Chicago, followed him to Washington, where not a few of those followers contrived to grow rich as the country grew poor, Mr. Seward attempted and did, many things which could scarcely be justified, but for which the administration was held responsible. It would be unjust to throw his eccentricities and errors upon others, and to award to him the honors and credit of successful measures of administration which he did not originate.

The President, never unreasonably obstinate or wilful, was ever lenient and forbearing, even when his intentions were defeated, and sometimes yielded to proceedings that his judgment did not fully approve. In the generosity of his nature he was tolerant of acts where a more arbitrary and imperious mind would have been implacable and unforgiving. There were occasions, however, when, relying on his own convictions, and the exigency being great, he exercised the executive will—the one-man power—with intelligent determination and effect. His promptness and energy in an emergency were displayed on one memorable occasion, when danger was imminent and immediate decision necessary. It may be mentioned as illustrative of his executive ability, promptness, and self-reliance; for it was in the absence of Mr. Seward, and when those on whom he had a right to rely failed him and were despondent. Gloom and national disaster were upon the country, but the President met the crisis with firmness, rose with the exigency, and independent of his Cabinet and against the general sentiment of the people, and by a sacrifice of personal feeling, adopted a course which results justified, and proved his ability as a chief.

In the early period of the war the proceedings and operations of the military commanders were unsatisfactory, and nowhere equalled the general expectation. Too much was doubtless expected and too little accomplished. None were more disappointed or depressed by the slow progress made than the President himself. For a period he had hopes from McClellan, whose talents at organization were displayed to advantage when, in the summer of 1861, he took command at Washington, established order, and enforced good military administration. In some respects the President esteemed him to be superior to any of the generals with whom he had come in contact; but the autumn and winter wore away in dilatory parades. With the change in the War Department in January, 1862, came the hostility of Secretary Stanton to McClellan, then General-in-Chief. The hesitating movements of that officer weakened the confidence of the President in his energy and military power. He still believed, however, that the general had superior military capacity and intelligence, but that he was inert, infirm of purpose; not quite ready to do all that he had the ability to accomplish. He required pushing, and the President therefore took upon himself to order a forward movement of both the army and navy. But McClellan continued tardy, and the winter and spring delays, followed by the sluggish movements on the York Peninsula and the reverses before Richmond, discouraged and greatly disheartened not only the President but the whole country. At this juncture, when, with large armies under him, he had more than he could perform in the line of his profession, McClellan in July wrote from his headquarters a very injudicious, not to say, impertinent letter to the President, in relation to the civil administration and the political conduct of affairs. This unwise letter, and the reverses of the army, with the active hostility of Stanton, brought Halleck, a vastly inferior man, to Washington. General Pope had preceded him, and, by an executive order creating the Army of Virginia, had been placed in command of the forces then in front of Washington, to the infinite disgust of some of the older generals. This disgust was increased by his public gasconading proclamation reflecting on the proceedings of his seniors—on their "lines of retreat and bases of supplies," which must, he said, thenceforward be discarded. These blatant bulletins, instead of inspiriting the men, caused ridicule in the ranks. The soldiers were attached to their old officers, particularly to McClellan, and to a great extent sympathized with him and other generals in their dislike, almost contempt, of this junior commander. Pope had been brought from the West directly after Halleck reported he had accomplished extraordinary achievements—reports grossly untrue, and which Pope himself afterward refuted. On coming to Washington, Pope, who was ardent, and I think courageous, though not always discreet, very naturally fell into the views of Secretary Stanton, who improved every opportunity to denounce McClellan and his hesitating policy. Pope also reciprocated the commendations bestowed on him by Halleck, by uniting with Stanton and General Scott in advising that McClellan should be superseded, and Halleck placed in charge of military affairs at Washington. This, combined with the movements and the disasters before Richmond, and his own imprudent letter, enabled Stanton to get rid of McClellan at headquarters. One of the first orders of Halleck on reaching Washington, after superseding McClellan, was for the withdrawal of the Army of the Potomac from the vicinity of Richmond. This recalled McClellan and his generals with their commands to the assistance of Pope, for whom they not only entertained no special regard, but some of them absolute hate. The orders to reinforce and assist Pope were consequently not obeyed with alacrity. There is no denying the fact that professional pride was allowed to encroach on patriotic duty in that momentous period. The selection of Pope to command that army may have been injudicious; he may not have been the man to take in hand and wield the immense force which met Lee and Jackson at the front; there may have been error on the part of Stanton and Halleck as well as Pope in slighting some of the older generals; the enmity of the Secretary of War toward McClellan may not without reason have been felt by him and his favorites as unjust; yet the welfare of the Republic should not have been put in jeopardy to gratify personal, official, or professional resentments. The general in command, whether young or old, should at such a crisis have been earnestly and in good faith sustained. Had that been the case, the results of the second battle at Manassas or Bull Run might have been different. But Pope was defeated, and the army, sadly demoralized, came retreating to the Potomac. The War Department, and especially Stanton and Halleck, became greatly alarmed. On the 30th of August, in the midst of these disasters and before the result had reached us, though most damaging information in regard to McClellan, who lingered at Alexandria, was current, the Secretary of the Treasury, Mr. Chase, called upon me with a protest, signed by himself and Stanton, denouncing the conduct of McClellan and demanding his immediate dismissal. Two other members were ready to append their names after mine. I declined to sign the paper, which was in the handwriting of Stanton, not that I did not disapprove of the course of the general, but because the combination was improper and disrespectful to the President, who had selected his Cabinet to consult and advise with, not to conspire against him; besides, some of the charges or allusions in the paper I knew nothing of, and I had doubted the wisdom of recalling the Army of the Potomac from Richmond, therein differing from Chase and Stanton. The object in bringing that army back to Washington in order to start anew, march overland, and regain the abandoned position, I did not understand unless it was to get rid of McClellan; and if that was the object, it would have been much better to place another general at the head of the army while it was yet on the James. But a majority of the Cabinet finally united in this proceeding. On Monday, the 1st of September, the paper, somewhat modified and signed by four of the Cabinet officers, was brought me. Mr. Seward was at the time absent from Washington—I never doubted purposely absent—and not of the number. My refusal and perhaps my remarks prevented the matter from proceeding further. The indignation against McClellan was at the time intense in Washington and the country. The President never knew of this paper, but was not unaware of the popular feeling against that officer in which he sympathized, and of the sentiments of the members of the Cabinet, aggravated by the hostility and strong, if not exaggerated rumors sent out by the Secretary of War. Both Stanton and Halleck were, however, filled with apprehensions beyond others, as the army of stragglers and broken battalions on the last of August and first of September came rushing toward Washington.

At the stated Cabinet meeting on Tuesday, the 2d of September, while the whole community was stirred up and in confusion, and affairs were gloomy beyond anything that had previously occurred, Stanton entered the council-room a few moments in advance of Mr.

Lincoln and said, with great excitement, he had just learned from General Halleck that the President had placed McClellan in command of the forces in Washington. The information was surprising, and, in view of the prevailing excitement against that officer, alarming. The President soon came in, and in answer to an inquiry from Mr. Chase, confirmed what Stanton had stated. General regret was expressed, and Stanton with some feeling remarked, that no order to that effect had issued from the War Department. The President, calmly but with some emphasis, said the order was his, and he would be responsible for it to the country. With a retreating and demoralized army tumbling in upon us, and alarm and panic in the community, it was necessary, the President said, that something should be done, but there seemed to be no one to do it. He therefore had directed McClellan, who knew this whole ground, who was the best organizer in the army, whose faculty was to organize and defend, and who would here act upon the defensive, to take this defeated and shattered army and reorganize it. He knew full well the infirmities of McClellan, who was not an affirmative man; was worth little for an onward movement; but beyond any other officer he had the confidence of the army, and he could more efficiently and speedily reorganize it and put it in condition than any other general. If the Secretary of War, or any member of the Cabinet, would name a general that could do this as promptly and well, he would appoint him. For an active fighting general he was sorry to say McClellan was a failure; he had "the slows"; was never ready for battle, and probably never would be; but for this exigency, when organization and defence were needed, he considered him the best man for the service, and the country must have the benefits of his talents though he had behaved badly. The President said he had seen and given his opinion to General Halleck, who was still General-in Chief; but Halleck had no plan or views of his own, proposed to do nothing himself, and fully approved his calling upon McClellan.

In stating what he had done the President was deliberate, but firm and decisive. His language and manner were kind and affectionate, especially toward two of the members who were greatly disturbed; but every person present felt that he was truly the chief, and every one knew his decision, though mildly expressed was as fixed and unalterable as if given out with the imperious command and determined will of Andrew Jackson. A long discussion followed, closing with acquiescence in the decision of the President, but before separating the Secretary of the Treasury expressed his apprehension that the reinstatement of McClellan would prove a national calamity.

In this instance the President, unaided by others, put forth with firmness and determination the executive will—the one-man power—against the temporary general sense of the community as well as of his Cabinet; two of whom it has been generally supposed had with him an influence almost as great as the Secretary of State. They had been ready to make issue and resign their places unless McClellan was dismissed; but yet knowing their opposition, and in spite of it and of the general dissatisfaction in the community, the President had in that perilous moment exalted him to new and important trusts. In an interview with the President on the succeeding Friday, when only he and myself were present, he unburthened his mind freely. Military matters were still in confusion, without plan or purpose at headquarters. The Secretary of War, under Pope's defeat and McClellan's reinstatement, was not only disappointed, but dejected and dispirited. The President said most of our troubles grew out of military jealousies. Whether changing the plan of operations (discarding McClellan and placing Pope in command in front) was wise or not, was not now the matter in hand. These things, right or wrong, had been done. If the administration had erred, the country should not have been made to suffer nor our brave men been cut down and butchered. Pope should have been sustained, but he was not. These personal and professional quarrels came in. Whatever may have been said to the contrary, it could not be denied that the army was with McClellan. He had so skilfully handled his troops in not getting to Richmond as to retain their confidence. The soldiers certainly had not transferred their confidence to Pope. He could, however, do no more good in this quarter. It was humiliating, after what had transpired and all we knew, to reward McClellan and those who failed to do their whole duty in the hour of trial, but so it was. Personal considerations must be sacrificed for the public good. He had kept aloof from the dissensions that prevailed, and intended to; "but," said he, "I must have McClellan to reorganize the army and bring it out of chaos. There has been a design, a purpose in breaking down Pope, without regard to the consequences to the country that is atrocious. It is shocking to see and know this, but there is no remedy at present. McClellan has the army with him." These were the views and this the course of the President when there was general dismay in the country and confusion in the army; the rebels near the intrenchments of Washington, and some of the Cabinet alarmed and preparing to leave. The President was not insensible to the deficiencies or ignorant of the faults of McClellan, nor yet blind to, and stubborn as regarded his better qualities. In placing him at the head of the army he went counter to the wishes of his friends, and forgetful of all else he subdued every personal feeling, and in the spirit of unselfish patriotism resolved to do what was for the true interest of the country. Had the general followed up the battle of Antietam, which took place a fortnight later, he would have retrieved the misfortunes of the peninsula and given the President additional reason to congratulate himself on the reinstatement; but the old dilatory infirmity remained, which strengthened the influence that persistently opposed him, and soon after led to his being retired from the command of the army.

THE President was a much more shrewd and accurate observer of the characteristics of men—better and more correctly formed an estimate of their power and capabilities—than the Secretary of State or most others. Those in the public service he closely scanned, but was deliberate in forming a conclusion adverse to any one he had appointed. In giving or withdrawing confidence he was discriminating and just in his final decision; careful never to wound unnecessarily the sensibilities of any for their infirmities, always ready to praise, but nevertheless firm and resolute in discharging the to him, always painful duty of censure, reproof, or dismissal.

Dupont he classed in the naval service with McClellan in the military. Both were intelligent, accomplished, and valuable officers in their way, but neither was the man for fierce encounter and desperate fighting. The two until tried had his support and all the confidence to which they were entitled, or which either had reason to expect. If the results at Port Royal were not followed up with the energy and vigor anticipated, the fault was, he justly considered, as much with the military as with the navy. But in the autumn of 1862 and winter of 1863 extensive preparations were made for retaking Fort Sumter and the capture of Charleston. Dupont visited Washington in the autumn, and had consulted on the subject, but would listen to no suggestion that any other officer should be detailed for that especial service, which he claimed as a right and as within the limits of his blockade. Extraordinary efforts were accordingly made by the Navy Department, which gave him a large portion of the best officers and vessels in the service that he might be successful. But time wore on, with no more effective demonstration than had been made by the army of the Potomac on the York peninsula. Dupont, like McClellan, was constantly asking for more reinforcements, and the Navy Department strained every nerve to aid him, and often answered his requisitions at the expense of other squadrons.

The President, as well as the whole country, felt greatly interested in this subject; not that Charleston was of any great strategic importance, but it was the hot-bed of secession, and there the rebellion had its origin. It was winter or early spring, and nothing had been accomplished, when the President one day said to me he had but slight expectation that we should have any great success from Dupont. "He, as well as McClellan," said Mr. Lincoln, "hesitates— has 'the slows.' McClellan always wanted more regiments; Dupont is everlastingly asking for more gunboats—more iron-clads. He will do nothing with any. He has intelligence and system, and will maintain a good blockade. You did well in selecting him for that command, but he will never take Sumter or get to Charleston. He is no Farragut, though unquestionably a good routine officer, who obeys orders and in a general way carries out his instructions." A few weeks served to verify all that the President had said on the subject. Dupont died without planting the flag on Sumter or visiting Charleston.

The views, theories and policy of Mr. Seward so far as he had a policy in relation to secession, were at the beginning different from the purposes and intentions of the President and his colleagues in the Cabinet. Through the winter of 1861 he possessed extraordinary opportunities to inform himself of the schemes and intrigues of the secessionists, and also the operations and designs of the Buchanan Administration as well as of the Republicans. In the Senate he had free intercourse with all parties, and the fact, well understood, that he was to receive the first appointment in Mr. Lincoln's Cabinet gave to his opinions weight and influence. Leading men of opposing factions courted and consulted him, for many, like Mr. Adams, underestimated the capacity and qualities of Mr. Lincoln, and assumed that the future Secretary of State would be the guiding spirit of the incoming administration. It is now well-known that Mr. Stanton, at that time a member of Mr. Buchanan's Cabinet was impressed with this belief and secretly confided to Mr. Seward the consultations and purposes of that administration. General Scott also, an old courtier as well as soldier, turned to the rising sun and in deference to the new projected policy, abandoned his original and sensible patriotic advice to Mr. Buchanan to garrison the southern forts and prepare the government for the threatened outbreak. Neither Mr. Lincoln nor any of his Cabinet except Mr. Seward, was aware of the schemes which had been maturing for a few months preceding the inauguration. Mr. Seward, with whom many of the southern leaders held intercourse, was gratified with the attention shown him, and, having really no settled convictions was kindly conciliatory and made concessions and promises which he found it difficult to carry fully into effect. In his speech of the 12th of January he expressed his intention " to meet exaction with concession," and his readiness to change the Constitution to get over difficulties. It has also been claimed and

9*

never denied, while facts go far to confirm the statement, that he had an understanding with the secessionists to the effect that Sumter and other forts in the seceding states should be surrendered. In such a purpose he entertained no intention of permanent disunion, but there are many circumstances which indicate that he contemplated temporary separation, and a reunion by a national convention to revise the constitution, and among other things give new guaranties to the slave-holding states. A new faith in expedients such as in the absence of principle had been resorted to by the Albany lobby and made successful in great emergencies.

On the 10th of April, two days after sending to Judge Campbell "Faith as regards Sumter—wait and see," he wrote to Mr. Adams: "Only an imperial or despotic government would subjugate thoroughly disaffected and insurrectionary members of the state. This federal republican system of ours is, of all forms of government, the very one which is most unfitted for such a labor. Happily however, this is only an imaginary defect. The system has, within itself adequate peaceful, conservative and recuperative forces. Firmness on the part of the government in maintaining and preserving the public institutions and property, and in executing the laws *where authority can be exercised without waging war*, combined with such measures of justice, moderation, and forbearance as will disarm reasoning opposition, will be sufficient to secure the public safety until returning reflection, concurring with the fearful experience of social evils, the inevitable fruits of faction, shall *bring the recusant mem-*

bers cheerfully back into the family, which, after all, must prove their best and happiest, as it undeniably is their most natural home. The Constitution of the United States provides for that return by authorizing Congress, on application to be made by a certain majority of the States, to *assemble a National Convention, in which the organic law can, if it be needful, be revised so as to remove all real obstacles to a reunion* so suitable to the habits of the people, and so eminently conducive to the common safety and welfare."

This was the scheme, or policy if it may be so called, of Mr. Seward and his conferees at the beginning, but it was not the policy of Mr. Lincoln. The letter to Mr. Adams was prepared, it will be remembered, at the very time when the squadron to relieve Fort Sumter was rendered abortive, by his detaching the Powhatan, the flag-ship from the expedition. Mr. Lincoln was not a party to the arrangements. They were concerted and employed to defeat his efforts to use the power of the government to check and break down the early movements of the rebels. The national forces and authority were ejected from the forts in South Carolina and Georgia. The "wayward sisters were to go in peace," and be brought back by a National Convention, " in which the organic law can be revised, so as to remove all real obstacles to a *reunion*."

Without discussing the soundness of the policy indicated in this letter to Mr. Adams and the facts which accord with that policy, it is sufficient to state, and subsequent events demonstrate, that it was not the policy of Mr. Lincoln, and the administration. In its details the course proposed by Mr. Seward conformed to the policy of Buchanan and Black, that a state could not be coerced—the union was to be dismembered and reunited by a new, or revised constitution. In these proceedings, Mr. Seward perplexed, confused and embarrassed, but did not direct affairs of the administration.

THE distinctive measure of Mr. Lincoln's Administration, beyond all others, that which makes it an era in our national history, is the decree of Emancipation. This movement, almost revolutionary, was a step not anticipated by him when elected, and which neither he nor any of his Cabinet was prepared for, or would have assented to when they entered upon their duties. He and they had, regardless of party discipline, resisted the schemes for the extension of slavery into free territory under the sanction of federal authority. All of them, though of different parties, were and ever had been opposed to slavery, but not one of them favored any interference with it by the National Government in the states where it was established or permitted. The assumption, after the acquisition of territory from Mexico, that slavery was a national and not a local institution had opened a new controversy in American politics, which contributed to the disintegration of old party organizations, each of which became in a measure sectional. The dissenting elements resisted the centralizing claim that slavery was national, not local; and ultimately, after a struggle of several years, they threw off old party allegiance and combined under a new organization, thenceforward known as Republican. In the first stages of this movement neither Mr. Lincoln nor Mr. Seward participated. Both of them had sympathized with what was known as the Free-soil party in 1848, but declined to become identified with it. They were politicians, and not then prepared to abandon the organization with which they had previously acted. Mr. Lincoln, with the free thought and independence of the men of the West, less trained and bound to party than the disciplined politicians in the old states, holding no official position, a quiet but observing and reflecting citizen; truthful, honest, faithful to his convictions, and with the mental strength and courage to avow and maintain them, early appreciated the important principles involved in this rising question, and boldly cast off the shackles of party in defence of the right, and earnestly, irrespective of any and all parties, opposed the extension and aggressions of slavery. Mr. Seward was in those days in office, trammelled by party followers and party surroundings. Trained during his whole public career in the severest discipline of party, indebted to it for his high position, always subservient to its decrees and requirements, active and exacting in enforcing its obligations, he had not the independence and moral stamina to free himself from the restraints and despotism of party, whatever were his sympathies, until the Whig organization disbanded. The people of the West, who knew Mr. Lincoln and appreciated his capabilities, tried in 1856 to place him on the ticket with Fremont as a candidate for Vice-President. Although but slightly known in the East, such was the zeal and enthusiasm in his favor of those who knew him, that nothing but the expediency of selecting an Eastern man to be associated with Fremont, who was from the West, prevented his nomination instead of Dayton. From the start he was a prominent Republican champion and leader, while Mr. Seward, a partisan politician, held off; was reluctant to leave the party with which he had been associated, hoping to make the new movement subservient to, or a part of the Whig party. Mr. Lincoln had no such purpose; the principles involved were with him above mere party. With no fortune, unaided by metropolitan funds or pecuniary assistance from any quarter, he gave his time and mind with unstinted devotion to the cause of freedom and in his memorable campaign with Douglass, alone and unassisted, he, through the empire State of the West, met the Senatorial giant on the questions of the extension of slavery, the rights of the states, the grants to and limitation of the powers of the general government, and displayed ability and power which won the applause of the country, and drew from Douglass himself expressions of profound respect.

When the Republicans, in convention at Chicago, chose their standard-bearer, they wisely and properly selected as their representative, the sincere and able man who had no great money-power in his interest, no disciplined lobby, no host of party followers, but who, like David, confided in the justice of his cause and with the simple weapons of truth and right, met the Goliath of slavery aggression, before assembled multitudes, in many a well-contested debate. The popular voice was not in error, or its confidence misplaced, when it selected and elected Lincoln.

After his election, and after the war commenced, events forced upon him the emancipation of the slaves in the rebellious states. It was his own act, a bold step, an executive measure originating with him, and was, as stated in the memorable appeal at the close of the final Proclamation, invoking for it the considerate judgment of mankind, warranted alone by military necessity. He and the Cabinet were aware that the measure involved high and fearful responsibility, for it would alarm the timid everywhere, and alienate, at least for a time, the bold in the border states who clung to the Union. The act itself could not have been justified or excused, and would never have been attempted, had the country been at peace; yet the movement seemed aggravated and more hazardous from the fact that the Union was weakened and imperilled by civil war. Results have proved that there was in the measure profound thought, statesmanship, courage, and far-seeing sagacity—consummate executive and administrative ability, which was, after some reverses, crowned with success. The nation, emerging from gloom and disaster, and the whole civilized world, united in awarding honor and gratitude to the illustrious man who had the mind to conceive and the courage and firmness to decree the emancipation of a race. Ten years after this event, when the patriot and philanthropist who decreed emancipation had been years in his grave, an attempt is made on a solemn occasion to award to one of his subordinates the honor and credit which justly belong to the great chief who decreed it. The Albany "Memorial Address" dwells on public measures, particularly during the war, but makes no allusion to this great act of Lincoln, nor to his merits in the cause of freedom, for which he labored and in which he died, but declares that his Secretary of State, a life-long partisan politician, was always opposed to slavery, and that he "directed affairs for the benefit of the nation, through the name of another." It is unnecessary, after what has already been said, to comment on this assumed direction by a subordinate instead of the chief, or on the gross injustice to Mr. Lincoln; but it should be known that the Secretary of State neither originated nor directed the affairs of the government on the great measure of emancipation. Mr. Seward was undoubtedly opposed to slavery, and so was every member of the administration, but his opposition never led him to propose any measure of relief to the country, or to take any steps against slavery which would be likely to impair the Whig party or the Whig organization while it existed. No specific act of his—no measure or distinct proposition to emancipate the slaves at any time—is mentioned, for there was none. In the administration of the government he took no advance step on the slavery question. Mr. Lincoln was the pioneer and responsible author, while the Secretary of State studiously avoided any expression of opinion in regard to it. The Secretaries of War and Navy were compelled to act in relation to fugitives from slavery who sought protection under the Union flag—an anomalous question—but they could obtain no counsel or advice from the Secretary of State how to act. He not only avoided giving an opinion, but recommended that the administration should abstain from any decisive stand on that controverted and embarrassing subject.

The President, who is represented as incompetent for his position, and whose mind in 1861, it is said, "had not even opened to the crisis," was reluctant to meddle with this disturbing element. Yet earlier than others he rightly appreciated what the government would have to encounter, and was convinced it must be taken in hand and disposed of. The magnitude of the rebellion, and the nature of the contest, compelled him, after the civil war had been carried on for twelve months, to grapple with this formidable subject. His first movement, in March 1862, was cautious and deliberate, characterized by great prudence and forethought, and designed not to alarm the friends of the Union by any harsh or offensive proceeding. It was an ameliorated plan for the gradual abolition of slavery by action of the states respectively, with the coöperation and assistance of the general government. This plan of voluntary and compensated emancipation was pressed upon Congress and the border slave states, with great earnestness, by the President. Mr. Blair and Mr. Bates, both residents of the border slave states, were the only members of the Cabinet who cordially seconded these first early measures in the cause of emancipation. Their associates cheerfully assented to and acquiesced in the proposition, but had neither faith nor zeal in its success; nor did Mr. Seward or any one of them suggest a different or more available plan for national relief. The subject was beset on every side with difficulty, requiring for its manipulation and disposition the highest order of administrative and executive ability. No one more than the President was impressed with the difficulties to be met, and at the same time with the imperative necessity of decisive action. The details of these proceedings, and the final determined stand taken by him—not by the Secretary of State or any of the Cabinet—to decree by an executive order the emancipation of the slaves in the rebellious states, have been elsewhere related. It was after all efforts for voluntary emancipation by the states interested, with pecuniary aid from the national treasury, had failed. To Mr Seward and myself the President communicated his purpose, and asked our views, on the 13th of July 1862. It was the day succeeding his last unsuccessful and hopeless conference with the representatives in Congress from the border slave states, at a gloomy period of our affairs, just after the reverses of our armies under McClellan before Richmond. The time, he said, had arrived when we must determine whether the slave element should be for or against us. Mr. Seward, represented as a superior in "native intellectual power," and as having forty years previously chosen his side, and as at that early period having claimed "a right in the government to emancipate slaves," was appalled and not prepared for this decisive step, when Mr. Lincoln made known to us that he contemplated by an executive order, to emancipate the slaves. Startled with so broad and radical a proposition, he informed the President that the consequences of such an act were so momentous that he was not prepared to advise on the subject without further reflection.

He had, it will be remembered, only the preceding year, in his carefully prepared and studied speech of the 12th of January 1861, avowed a policy diametrically opposed to emancipation by the general government. "I am willing," said he, on that occasion, "to vote for an amendment to the Constitution declaring that it shall not by any future amendment be so altered as to confer on Congress a power to abolish or interfere with slavery in any state." In addition to this speech on the floor of the Senate and in corroboration of it, he, as a member of the Senatorial committee of thirteen, proposed the following amendment to the Federal Constitution : "No amendment shall be made to the Constitution, which will authorize or give to Congress any power to abolish or interfere in any state with the domestic institutions thereof, including that of persons held to service or labor by the laws of said state."

The President aware of the position taken by Mr. Seward and of the embarrassment which he might feel in acceding to a measure that conflicted with that position, stated he wished from neither of us a committal, but he thought best to make known to us, that emancipation appeared to him an inevitable necessity.

While Mr. Seward hesitated, and had the subject under consideration, the President deliberately prepared his preliminary proclamation, which met the approval, or at least the acquiescence, of the whole Cabinet, though there were phases of opinion not entirely in accord with the proceedings. Mr. Blair, an original emancipationist, and committed to the principle, thought the time to issue the order inopportune, and Mr. Bates desired that the deportation of the colored race should be coincident with emancipation. Aware that there were shades of difference among his counsellors, and hesitation and doubt with some, in view of the vast responsibility and its consequences, the President devised his own scheme, held himself alone accountable for the act, and, unaided and unassisted, prepared each of the proclamations of freedom. Mr. Seward in no way or form originated or was responsible for that important measure, did not in any way "direct affairs" in regard to it, was in no other way cognizant of it beyond his colleagues, except as communicated to him and myself on the 13th of July, at its inception. Yet in the "Memorial Address," Mr. Seward is represented as the life-long opponent of slavery, beyond others the master spirit in the Lincoln Administration. The President and this great event are ignored, and the inference is intended to be conveyed, that the Secretary of State who " chose his side" in the morning of life adverse to slavery, is entitled to the credit; for it is represented that the President was a mere secondary personage, and the Secretary of State directed affairs in the name of Mr. Lincoln, who was to "reap the honors due chiefly to Mr. Seward's labors."

To unfold the leaves of suppressed history, and correct the errors and perversions which interested—and many of them still living—persons have spread abroad and inculcated, is a thankless task, and will subject him who performs it to partisan abuse. It is scarcely to be expected that the present generation will know or be able to appreciate the labors and acts of those who, intrusted with the government in a trying period, took upon themselves immense and unprecedented responsibilities, or that a rightful discrimination will at this early day, if ever, be made as regards those who in the quiet of civil official life participated in the movements which eventuated in the salvation of the Union and the emancipation of a race. The late labored effort of the distinguished gentleman of an historic family and name to depreciate the talents and services of Abraham Lincoln, and to crown another with honors that justly belong to him, is a specimen of lamentable partisan prejudice and error. It is but one, and perhaps the last of many attempts of a similar character, to take from the brow of Lincoln the wreath of merit that is justly his—to deprive him of the reward due for his labor, and give to another credit for his acts. It is not the first time in our history when like injustice has been witnessed toward our Chief Magistrates. Volumes have been written to prove that Hamilton controlled Washington and directed the affairs of the nation in the name of his chief. Van Buren, it was claimed, controlled the imperious will of Jackson and dictated his measures. Undoubtedly each had influence with his chief, perhaps more than he deserved. The same may be said of Mr. Seward, who had undeniably influence with Mr. Lincoln, but who was no more the directing mind of the Administration of Lincoln, but really much less, than was Hamilton of Washington or Van Buren of Jackson. Both Hamilton and Seward are charged with having given countenance to this false impression, which, however, redounds to the credit of neither.

In these pages written to correct the misconceptions of Mr. Adams, and the misrepresentations of the Albany "Memorial Address," incidents of what occurred would, I thought, better than mere contradictory assertions, illustrate the acts, the executive management and administrative ability, as well as the capacity and mental energy of the men whose traits are involved in the statements which have been made.

Of the incidents that took place during the administration of Mr. Lincoln, some of which and the attending circumstances could not have been disclosed at the time of their occurrence, there are in most cases living witnesses. The transactions of an earlier date are of public notoriety and matters of record, commencing with the organized anti-masonic proscription, and embracing the rise and fall of that and subsequent parties, down to, and including the much misrepresented proceedings of the Chicago Convention in 1860.

It has been no part of my purpose to magnify or overstate the qualities, or to give undue credit to the labors and abilities of Mr. Lincoln, still less to do injustice to Mr. Seward, who is represented in the "Memorial Address" as overshadowing his chief. Mr. Lincoln was in many respects a remarkable, though I do not mean to say an infallible man. No true delineation or photograph of his intellectual capacity and attributes has ever been given, nor shall I attempt it. His vigorous and rugged, but comprehensive mind, his keen and shrewd sagacity, his intellectual strength and mental power, his genial, kindly temperament—with charity for all and malice towards none— his sincerity, unquestioned honesty and homely suavity, made him popular as well as great. Had he survived to this day, the Albany "Memorial Address" would have been of a different character, and its pages not marred with paragraphs which reflect on his ability and do injustice to his memory.

THE END.

www.ingramcontent.com/pod-product-compliance
Lightning Source LLC
Chambersburg PA
CBHW031829230426
43669CB00009B/1279